D1213698

Read the
Wild Water

Read the Wild Water

780 Miles by Canoe Down the Green River

by Robert Franklin Leslie

*Illustrated
with Photographs*

351689

E. P. DUTTON & CO., INC.   New York

To
my wife,
Lea Rochat Leslie

Copyright © 1966 by Robert Franklin Leslie
All rights reserved. Printed in the U.S.A.
No part of this book may be reproduced in any form
without permission in writing from the publisher,
except by a reviewer who wishes to quote brief passages
in connection with a review written
for inclusion in a magazine, newspaper or broadcast.
Published simultaneously in Canada by
Clarke, Irwin & Company Limited, Toronto and Vancouver
Library of Congress catalog card number: AC 66–10324

FIRST EDITION

The photographs in this book are reproduced through the cour-
tesy of Robert Franklin Leslie, excepting those on pages 109,
(bottom), 114, and 180, which are reproduced through the cour-
tesy of Michael A. Kem.

Contents

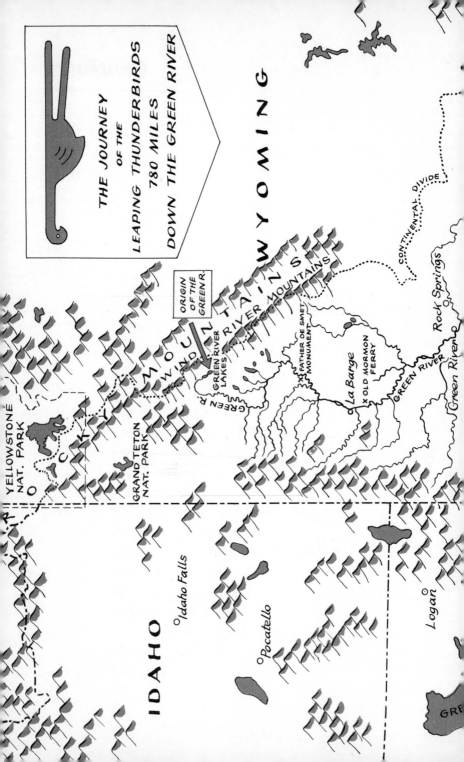

THE JOURNEY
OF THE
LEAPING THUNDERBIRDS
780 MILES
DOWN THE GREEN RIVER

WYOMING

WIND RIVER MOUNTAINS

ROCKY MOUNTAINS

ORIGIN OF THE GREEN R.

GREEN RIVER LAKES

GREEN R.

CONTINENTAL DIVIDE

Rock Springs

Green River

GREEN RIVER

X FATHER DE SMET MONUMENT

La Barge

X OLD MORMON FERRY

YELLOWSTONE NAT. PARK

GRAND TETON NAT. PARK

IDAHO

°Idaho Falls

°Pocatello

Logan°

GRE

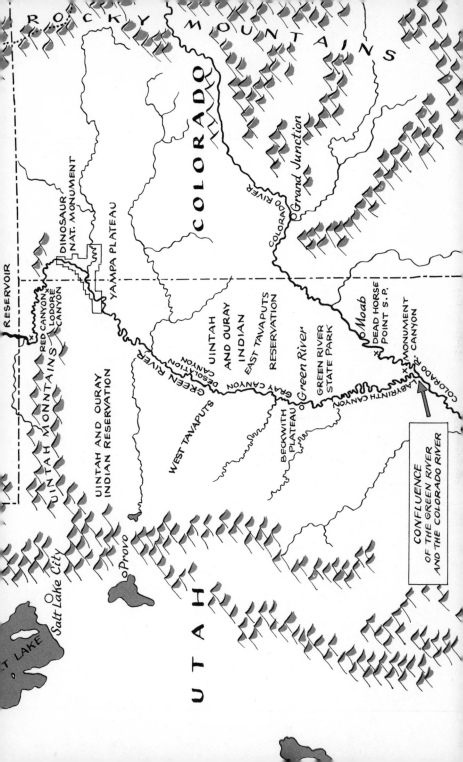

I

Green River Challenge

On the afternoon of July fifteenth I parked the station wagon at the site of the old Mormon Ferry near La Barge, Wyoming. Seven boys and I climbed a barren hill from whose crest we stared in silent wonder up and down the vast flood plain of the mighty Green River. We were determined to canoe the turbulent stream's seven-hundred-eighty miles of uncertain wilderness between Green River Lake and the Colorado River. No one had ever succeeded in canoeing the full length of the Green.

At length I suggested, "It's not too late to change our minds. We can continue north and do the Columbia instead—much safer."

"I'm not chicken," Mike Kem said. "Just admiring it."

"Let's get on up to that lake and start down before I back out," Mike Laine added.

We spoke very little during the remaining seventy-five miles to Cora. Cora, Wyoming, listed on road maps as a town, consisted of one small general store where we bought a two-weeks' supply of food.

Beyond Cora the gravel road leading to the lake deteriorated rapidly. The final fifteen miles beyond the last ranch was barely negotiable for a loaded station wagon pulling a trailer full of gear and four canoes. The so-called road was little more than two muddy ruts with chug holes and booby traps. It was the kind of road fishermen like to follow to jackpot pools because they know they won't have to compete with a crowd at the other end.

What the dreadful road left to be desired, however, was more than repaid in the magnificence of the Wind River Mountains. The Green River, wandering emerald green and swift through wide, luxuriant meadows where herds of elk, deer, and antelope were grazing, flowed parallel with the road. As we turned into the mouth of the terminal canyon for the final climb to the lake, we began to question our early confidence that we could get canoes through the miles of frothing white water we discovered there. The steep grade of the road gave us an approximate estimate of the speed of the water tumbling down that canyon.

Quite suddenly our route pitched into the eternal twilight of dense forest: lodgepole pine, firs, and impenetrable stands of white-skinned aspens. Precipitous 13,000-foot summits towered all around us. In the late afternoon light, glaciers and perpetual snowfields glistened like pearls around the neck of Gannett Peak, highest point in Wyoming.

At road's end we found no fishermen, but moose, elk, and deer ignored us as they browsed along both banks of a talkative little trout stream which passed through a small campground. Marmots and picas from their precarious hermitages high on avalanched moraines whistled back and forth across the canyon, and the canyon walls whistled back. Whisky jacks (Clark's nutcracker) and crested jays intimidated us for handouts. Squirrels and chipmunks soon skittered in for their share when they saw the birds eating from our hands. The primitive scene was one of cleanliness, friendly wild creatures, and uninitialed tree trunks.

Before unpacking, we all ran down the densely forested slope for a look at the willow-fringed Green River Lake. Every plant at water's edge—yarrow, senecio, marshmallow, buttercup, and columbine—seemed to be competing to outblossom its neighbor. Meadow bogs near the outlet were hip deep in grasses and sedges as brilliant as if their leaves had been varnished. Wild animals watched from all sides, and we couldn't breathe without inhaling a bird's song.

Here in majestic loneliness almost unknown, sparkled a glacial basin of water that, for sheer beauty and grandeur of setting, would rival any lake in America. Roaring cataracts entered from the upper end of the basin, draining Upper Green River Lake, which was equally as isolated and almost indistinguishable in appearance from its twin five hundred

---

Green River Lake, source of the Green River in Wyoming's Wind River Mountains, actual launching site of the trip. Continental Divide in background.

yards below. Both lakes are fed by runoff from the brood-
ing Dinwoody Glaciers along the Continental Divide less
than ten miles to the east. The Sacajawea-Fremont group
of peaks to the south also watershed the Green. We
counted twelve separate crags which rose in the form of a
jagged 13,000-foot horseshoe around the lakes. California's
Sierra Nevada is the only range on the North American
Continent to exceed Wyoming's Wind River Mountains
in number of 13,000-foot peaks.

Literally hundreds of small feeder lakes and streams
above the deep, somber wells of Green River Lakes, as well
as the larger Fremont, Willow, and New Fork Lakes and
their tributaries to the southwest, compose the complex
known as the headwaters of the upper Colorado River
drainage system which terminates in the Sea of Cortez
(Gulf of California) 2300 miles away. Like that of the
Mississippi system, the general course of the Green is from
north to south. The result of a geological accident—the
rise of a short, ridged dike, Fish Creek, which within a few
miles becomes the Gros Ventre (Fat Belly)—has its
source under a glacier less than five miles from the Green;
yet the Gros Ventre empties into the Pacific Ocean via the
Snake and the Columbia Rivers. The same Dinwoody
Glaciers which drape over both sides of the Continental
Divide above the Green River Lakes give rise to the Wind
River which empties into the Gulf of Mexico via the Big
Horn, the Missouri, and the Mississippi. Thus, conceiv-
ably, a single snowflake, falling on exactly the right alpine
tundra along the Continental Divide in Wyoming's Wind
River Mountains, could melt and share its flow equally
with two oceans by way of our three greatest river systems.

When we returned to camp, swarms of mosquitoes descended upon us, stinging all exposed parts of our bodies as well as through shirts and the tight parts of our jeans. Smoke fires of green sage and pine needles, however, finally drove most of the insects away.

The boys had begun to show signs of fatigue from prolonged excitement and the ride from Los Angeles. I was dead on my feet. After a simple supper of hot dogs, salad, and pineapple, we practically fell into our sleeping bags. By nine o'clock the night had become too chilly for mosquitoes, but other pests conspired to plague relaxation.

Listening to the gossipy little stream, I had barely fallen asleep when a gawky yearling bear rattled a stew pot off the table and helped himself to the prunes I had planned for breakfast. Deciding not to disturb the boys, I got up to have it out with the bear. The brute crossed the road and sat down against an alder while I inspected the damage. When I extinguished the flashlight, the party-crasher joined me at the table. At a distance of three feet I flashed the light directly into his face. Mumbling some ursine oath, he disappeared on the double, but when I cut the light, he returned.

I could have been an ungracious host and clubbed him out of camp, but the act would have been forever on my conscience, because the memory of that beating might later have turned him into a vicious bear. So I employed the old Canadian doublecross by pouring out a panful of dry oatmeal which would swell up in his stomach and satisfy most of his hunger until morning. He ate the cereal with great gusto and came near mauling me for more. I then poured a small cupful into the pan and gave it a generous sprinkling of black pepper. He sniffed, sneezed, tried to eat it, sneezed again, then slowly wandered away down the road, satisfied he had cleaned me out of every-thing edible; the pepper remaining in his nostrils probably precluded any further thought of food that night. It was comforting to have seen the last of that bear.

Sleep at last—or so I thought. No sooner had I closed my eyes than a loud thumping broke out down by the lake. Some varmint was using one of our canoes for a bass drum! Grabbing tennis shoes, flashlight, and an aspen shillelagh, I rushed to the boats.

Two bull moose with lowered antlers were facing each other; one shiny red canoe separated the snorting, black behemoths. The two opponents preferred to stand and argue and kick the aluminum craft rather than move eight feet either way to more adequate grounds for combat. They ignored me and my flashlight, probably because neither moose dared take his eyes off the other for so much as a side glance, out of respect for a possible ramming from his opponent's eighty-five-pound rack of antlers. Bull moose possess the heaviest horns in the animal kingdom.

My own panic grew with each passing moment lest one of the 2000-pound monsters suddenly step inside the canoe and pierce the hull with a sharp, splayed hoof. I couldn't just crouch there behind a tree and witness the destruction of a canoe. Suddenly remembering that my father had once said that a moose was afraid of nothing but fire, I rushed back up the hill to camp, grabbed some matches and a paper sack, and returned to the battlefield. Neither moose had budged an inch, and both were still thumping the canoe. Placing a small stone in the bottom of the sack, I ignited the dry paper and tossed it between the hind legs of the nearest animal. The hotfoot broke up the stalemate, but the canoe's custom paint job was pocked and dented.

Back in my sleeping bag once more, I began to reflect upon the events and issues that had brought about this trip.

Having canoed most of the great rivers of the West with boys, I had saved the Green for last due to widespread rumors of its treacherous nature. There existed precious little to read or find out other than the fact that no one had ever canoed it before.

The three Mikes—Mike Kem, Mike Laine, and Mike Shannon, a trio of thirteen-year-olds—had had no canoeing experience but did have an enthusiastic yen to learn. Chip Cobley, a stocky, burr-headed, sixteen-year-old, was also inexperienced though eager to learn. Joe Krahulik, Reese Milner, and Craig Close had proved their canoeing ability with me the year before on wilderness lakes and rivers in northwestern British Columbia. Craig, barely thirteen, went by the name of Little Wolf—"Little" because he didn't weigh eighty pounds, and "Wolf" because he had an insatiable appetite for any experience as long as it involved food and outdoor adventure.

Basically they satisfied all the requirements for a good crew: a vital interest in developing the keen senses necessary for survival camping, a genuine respect for every wild creature, and an inclination to cooperate without question under conditions of crisis and emergency. Each boy was eager to earn his share of the costs of the trip and bear an equal part of the daily work load.

I recalled also the solemn conferences with the boys' parents. Including my own private set of trepidations, I didn't whittle the truth about the Green River's built-in hazards. Their decisions to allow their sons to undertake the perilous journey was based either upon confidence in my long, accident-free experience on water or upon an unshakable faith in the Almighty.

Between the first of May and the fifteenth of July, we had spent every spare waking hour in feverish, minute preparation. I took delivery on four 15-foot, 78-pound Aluma-Craft aluminum canoes so as to begin the exciting job of painting and outfitting. We built six light-weight plywood grub boxes bolted all around with aluminum angles for strength. We haunted the surplus stores for tarps, nylon ropes, waterproof containers, sheet aluminum and rivets—anticipating the worst—and the many little "goodies" that spell the difference in wilderness camping.

One of the most important tools of our trade was paddles. Each of us ordered two straight-grained spruce blades, eight inches wide, with looms as long as the distance between chin and toes. Each paddle, weighing less than two pounds, was sanded glass smooth and given fifteen coats of marine deck varnish. We painted or inlaid insignia on the blades before varnishing.

The decision to buy Aluma-Craft instead of other equally fine aluminum canoes was predicated upon my former experience with this particular craft. We preferred the lines and construction of another manufacturer, the weight and speed of still another; but the width and fight ability of the Aluma-Craft determined the selection. The choice was not easy. Personally, I do not like the aluminum siffle, i.e., the sound of water against the moving canoe's hull, and I am reminded of kettle drums every time the metal thumps through choppy ripples. Yet from the standpoint of easy repairs on the spot, nothing can compete with aluminum.

For high visibility from the air in the event we might

have to be rescued, we painted two canoes bright poppy orange and two fire-engine red, using metal primer and two coats of marine enamel. For contrast, the orange craft received red gunnels and bang-strip trim, while the red ones were outlined in orange. Along both bows of each canoe we silver-stenciled our Flying Thunderbird emblem.

This design was handed down through my father's Cherokee Indian ancestry. The Cherokees applied the symbol to their fabulous birch rinds and pirogues in which hunting parties and war crews penetrated the swamps, lakes, bayous, and streams of the Carolinas and Georgia. The strangely stylized bird was supposed to see far ahead and thus pick a safe route for the braves. When Sequoyah became chief of the Cherokees and abandoned war as a means of settling differences, my father's people followed him to Arkansas and Texas where they found little use for canoes, but the spirit of the noble craft with the Flying Thunderbird emblems still haunts and taunts our imaginations to this very day.

Despite the bear and moose incidents and fatigue from the drive from California to Green River Lake, we were awake long before dawn. Breakfast over, Chip Cobley and Mike Kem drove the car down the road to meet the rest of us at the head of the first rapid. By making several trips by car along the road between the lake and Daniel village, we avoided having to load the canoes during those first miles. This would also give the boys much-needed experience in fast water without risking the loss of valuable equipment in the event of an upset. Little Wolf, Shannon, Laine, Krahulik, Milner, and I paddled three canoes from camp to the outlet.

After funneling from a north neck of the lake at a good clip, the Green River accelerated as it charged down the wide gorge, but there were no rapids during the first mile. In flood state because of recent rains and warm weather effects upon the snow fields, the current was faster and less maneuverable than it would have been under normal conditions. Along this stretch, Joe Krahulik was teaching Mike Laine some of the fine points of bowmanship; Craig Close did a similar job for Mike Shannon. Reese Milner and I took the lead to warn of rocks, whirlpools, deadfalls, or barbed-wire fences which stock ranchers frequently stretch across the river—a necessary evil. Within minutes we beached above the first rapid where Kem and Cobley had unloaded their canoe.

Assembling along the left bank, we were now ready to "read" the rapid, a mile-long stretch of boulder-strewn white water involving a bend in the river. "Reading" a rapid before running it results in the difference between successful passage, an icy spill, a variety of damages, or even drowning.

To "read the water" means beaching above a rapid's lip and walking down the bank to study the channels between obstructions. The decision to run a rapid or "string" the boats down near the shore by ropes is reached during reading. Location of exact point of entry, crossovers, suction tendencies of the current, deepest water, submerged boulders, and point of exit must be determined, and guidons established before attempting to run a cataract. In other words, the course through the entire length must be assiduously plotted, memorized, and adhered to. Disasters occur when people attempt to read the water from moving canoes.

Rapids are caused by narrow channels that have been partially filled with rocks from caved-in banks, by shallow spread-out of the river bed, by a sharp downward pitch of a canyon, or by some combination of these features. A rapid's geological history determines its characteristics. Ocean swells and waves move along until they reach a shore, while river waves remain stationary. The current moves over the rocks which cause the waves, but the frothy crests themselves stand disconcertingly still above the impediment. Before a stream surges into a rapid, there is always a calm, partially dammed pool which purls the water into the rough bed through a smooth, slick V, sometimes referred to as the arrowhead.

Most rapids are canoed by formula, yet each cataract with its own peculiarities may alter the sequences of that formula. In any event you don't have time to juggle theories during the needle-threading operation in and out among the boulders. Shooting rapids, like landing an airplane, is not learned through making mistakes.

For the sternman to realize steerage control or "purchase," the canoe must maintain slightly faster surface speed than the river current. This speed is attained in the calm water just before the V, and vigorous paddling must be continued throughout the entire length of the white water—and beyond—since the downstream tails of many rapids are characterized by treacherous whirlpools and "death holes." Strange as it may sound—but not so strange when you analyze human panic—the tendency of canoeists is to lose surface speed in a rapid.

"Follow the slick through the V on this one," I said as we walked back to the canoes. "Keep left of the crests and head for green water. Paddle ahead of the current. Pay no attention to the noise of the water, the siffle, or the kettle-drumming of the hull. Kneel on your rubber pads. Don't talk except to shout one-word commands: 'Left' or 'Right.' The bowman is in command in a rapid. You'll get splashed with ice water. Ignore it. Keep paddling. Like riding a bicycle, don't sit there and stare at a rock you want to miss. Cross over to the right bank before you get to that log jam and stay over there until you round the bend. Then cut back to the center and gradually work your way all the way over to the left bank. Don't try to beach until you're well beyond that whirlpool. Now all of you stand down there on that knoll above the bend and watch while Reese and I run it. Wait till we walk back, Joe, before you and Laine start down."

The boys stationed themselves at a point above the bend where they could see, and Reese Milner and I shoved off. We were hitting about four miles an hour faster than the current as we glided over the slick, sped down the V, and cataracted into the principal channel through the sluice between the first boulders.

Every move went according to formula until we reached the bend in the river. When we attempted to cross the fierce crests in order to get over to the right bank, we lost speed and began to sideslip down midstream. That could have brought on a roll with loss of canoe and a nasty dunking, so I swung her back to the left, shouted for Reese to dig in deeper with his paddle, and tried to maintain the tops of the crests down the big middle. As the bow rose over the first wave, the trough dumped twenty-five gallons of ice water into my lap.

"You still with me?" Reese shouted without looking back.

"Just barely! There's an opening to the left. Get between those two rocks." I was uncertain that Reese could understand me above the din and pitch of the wild water. We shot between the two boulders with nothing more than a noisy keel scrape, but beyond that point we were in for it. The suction from half the volume of the river pulled us down the wrong chute and toward the next boulder.

"Back water!" I howled. And a good thing we did. Had we not broken our speed, the canoe would have been destroyed when we crashed head-on into that rock. As it was, we took on another twenty-five gallons of water. Catapulting out of the canoe and onto the rock at the moment of impact, Reese seized the bow, swung her around into the sluice to the right of the boulder, and reboarded in half the time it takes to tell it. We were swamping fast and had to get ashore at all cost. Fortunately, beyond the big rock lay an embayment.

Out of nowhere Joe Krahulik appeared, up to his chest in the growling water. Grabbing the nylon painter, he anchored all his straining weight upstream, pivoted the sinking canoe 180 degrees, and let the current yaw us into the rocky bank.

"Shall we continue?" asked my dripping, shivering, cool-headed companion when the water had been dumped from the canoe. Reese had found delight in the fracas.

We resumed course according to original reading, beaching from a quiet eddy fifty yards below the whirlpool. As we hiked the road back to where the other boys waited, I expected and fully deserved a first-class razzing from the entire crew for my boober, but to this day they've never mentioned it.

Smiling like a fox that had just swallowed a setting of eggs but without taking his eyes from the river, Joe whispered, "I suppose we should cut over a little sooner."

"By all means!" I said. I could see how anxious he was to come to intimate quarters with the challenge.

Without further discussion, the rest of us stood on the promontory and watched Joe Krahulik and Mike Laine paddle with deliberate precision into the V. I gasped at the amount of daylight I saw between their keel and the water when they bounced off the first crest. Above the steady liquid roar we could hear the dull slap of the aluminum hull each time the canoe fell from crest to trough.

"Those hulls sound like thunder," Shannon remarked. "Look at those emblems leap. Leaping Thunderbirds!" And, for the rest of the trip, the canoes were called "Leaping Thunderbirds."

Joe nodded and smiled as they cleared the big log jam, shot full speed beyond the bend, and re-crossed toward the left bank. A wild "Bravo!" went up from all of us as the two boys closed with the beach below the "death hole."

Chip Cobley and Mike Kem held rigidly to formula for an almost perfect run. Mike Shannon and Craig Close were the smallest and youngest boys, but with Close's previous summer of Canadian experience, he gave to the Little Wolf–Shannon team an edge of canoeing candor and technique which surpassed the strength and maturity of the Kem–Cobley combination. Little Wolf never entered anything half-cocked. He always knew exactly what to do, and he did it. Shannon's eagerness to learn and willingness to work hard soon harnessed all his initial clumsiness.

The Green River's Round One Rapid. Mike Laine and Joe Krahulik have just entered the white water.

Driving the car two miles down the road to the second series of rapids, I allowed the boys to experiment in less dangerous current. I admonished them to read their water carefully, make their runs separately, beach often, and take no chances.

With all canoes ashore above the second stretch of rapids, we walked along the low banks to read the next water. For two additional miles there were intermittent runs of major rapids, some extremely dangerous, others just dangerous, there being no such article as a safe rapid.

Near the mouth of the canyon, the sloping sagebrush floor was half a mile wide, open, and unforested except for broken fringes of dwarf willow near the river. As the stream began its horseshoe bend out of the northern extremity of the Wind River Mountains in order to assume its general southerly course for the rest of its length, the mountains dropped abruptly behind. The landscape fanned out into long, gently inclining hills where herds of antelope, wapiti, and deer grazed in knee-deep timothy and wheat grass. Sparse stands of stately pines and scattered groves of giddy aspens crowned the southern hills on the side where the road was, but the northern inclines of the rapidly widening fan were exposed to frosty winds and therefore almost barren of trees.

"Looks as if we better do this one in sections," Joe proposed as we studied the complex of channels.

"A hundred yards at a time," Mike Shannon added, still shivering from a dunking he received during an uncoordinated, all-points landing at his last beaching.

For the next two miles the river dropped through a sequence of terraces. On level stretches the current passed through deep, even channels; but at intervals, when the stream stepped down the risers to the next level, the furious water bit savagely at dozens of exposed boulders and trapped deadfalls. Each terraced drop had to be read and run separately. Each section had its own tight formula for shooting, its own rigid law for survival of man and equipment. And we obeyed that law. Here indeed flowed a river with a character and personality of its own.

As it worked out, the Leaping Thunderbirds emerged with nothing worse than scraped keels and bottoms. Milner and I picked up a small side dent during a fraction of a second's indecision, while Kem and Cobley broke a drag pole in an attempt to beach parallel with a rocky shore.

We soon learned that any type of pole, dragged along the bottom of the stream for slowing down, especially during beaching or easing along through places otherwise too difficult to run, was impractical equipment against the innate violence of the Green. As a more satisfactory method of closing with the shore, the bowman simply shipped his paddle, moved onto the bow wedge, projected his feet forward, and absorbed the shock with his legs. From this position he could protect his bangstrip, jump ashore instantly, and hold the craft by the nylon painter attached to the bow ring through a hondo.

At the end of another mile of relatively smooth water, we assembled to read the succeeding three-mile series of up-enders facetiously known as Round Three—half a river wide and two and a half rivers fast. According to local river boatmen, anyone might luck out in Round One or Round Two; but Round Three should be portaged, in other words the canoes should be beached and carried around the worst water.

We debated the possibilities over peanut butter and ham sandwiches. Should we portage to the next still water and keep our skin, bones, and canoes the way they were, or should we flirt with danger just to be able to say we'd canoed every mile of the Green River?

Round Three reminded me of certain tantalizing runs on the upper Thompson and Fraser Rivers in British Columbia where my French-Canadian Beaver Indian friend, Alex Charbeau, and I used to shoot the rapids for the thrill of seeing how far we could go before being tossed out of the canoe or swamping. In those days we thought life jackets had been invented exclusively for "flatlanders," and we preferred to nurse our broken ribs, cracked noggins, and water-logged lungs rather than have our cynical friends on shore accuse us of being "sissy." Charbeau was an astute canoeist and a champion swimmer. Yet in a relatively

Mike Shannon, fore; Reese Milner, aft, shoot the turbulent crests of Round Three Rapid.

simple run down the Salmon River's Chair Creek Rapid near Riggins, Idaho, Charbeau met with an unnecessary accident. Runoff from late summer rains had silted the river, concealing a cluster of sub-surface rocks with which his canoe collided. He was *not* wearing a life jacket, and knocked unconscious, was drowned. The river never surrendered his body.

"The first lap doesn't look too bad," Cobley concluded when we discovered the first escape hatch on the right bank. At this point the boys were exhilarated by initial successes. Each challenge goaded them to boldness which could be admirable provided that boldness was tempered with prudence and respect.

"We'll run it by installments," I agreed. "Let's get the first section behind us before we even read the second. Reese, you and I'll lead off. If we make any mistakes, the rest of you know what to do."

From the trouncing we took during the first fifty yards, I

thought the hull's keel seam would surely split before we could get ashore. There was no pattern of rhythm in the beat of the waves or in the flow of the current. Even the meanest bucking bronco employs some natural rhythm. But not the Green in her Round Three Rapid. We could no more anticipate the approach of shock nor protect ourselves against it by planting our knees in the sponge rubber padding and bracing our rear ends against the edges of the seats than we could control the rise and fall of the bow. As each canoe came down, I could see the boys' heads whip-lashing as they struggled for balance and stabbed their blades hard into the crests for purchase and steerage. The second section was worse; but somehow we all ducked the punches by following an unerring, sequentially memoorized course.

I was for throwing in the towel after reading the third and final mile of Round Three. Once in, there was no escape, no beach for 1700 yards. There weren't as many exposed rocks as in some of the upper rapids, but the waterwheeling cockscombs were more frequent and more vicious, guaranteeing the rocks were there, all right, but submerged—"depth charges" just inches below our waterlines and impossible to detect because of the angle of bright sunlight on white froth.

Krahulik and Laine asked to try it first, so Little Wolf and I chose second place. Shannon and Milner did an unbelievably professional follow up. "Just bull luck," Shannon admitted.

We beached at the first possible shore and waited to photograph Kem and Cobley as they came down the home stretch. Milner gave them the signal to start.

From the first glimpse of the fourth canoe, we knew they

were in trouble. They were out of formula. Instead of forcing to the right bank, they began pitching the center boils and burbles, losing surface speed second by precious second. Chip, with all his strength, was unable to helm either to starboard or to port. The twenty-mile current sucked them into the exposed roots of a deadfall pine with such tremendous impact that both boys were flung like matchsticks into the raging deluge. Their canoe up-ended, hung momentarily like a long red feather on the next crest, rolled over and was gulped down the trough. The flotation styrofoam fore and aft, however, soon refloated the canoe.

By some miracle the boys were able to crawl back into the swamped craft to protect their bodies from the rocks to come. As the river buffeted them past us, we could only stare helplessly from the bank. What a sorry sight! Wet hats pulled down over their faces by overtight neck strings, paddles flying wildly against the hostile current to no avail. Fortunately they had remembered to keep a thwart-anchored length of nylon shroud line around the paddle looms to keep from losing them just in case something like this should happen.

"Get ashore!" I yelled, gesticulating with my arms. I could see that the canoe was too badly bent out of shape for maneuvering, but the boys refused to abandon ship.

"Let's follow with the car," suggested Joe, the only one of us who didn't appear to have lost his reason. "We can head them off and throw them a line."

I called up the last erg of my remaining strength and ran up the hill to the road. All I could think of was that next series of cackling, plummeting rapids below Round Three. Fifteen costly minutes were lost because my car wouldn't start.

"Hey! That's Kem coming up the road!" Milner said suddenly.

I couldn't be sure. Whoever we saw was a mile away. Some of us started off to meet him, while Joe continued to coax the engine. But for better or for worse, it *was* Mike Kem. He was minus his hat; his clothes were torn to shreds; he was dragging his life jacket and paddle; he was bruised, bleeding, limping, slobbering, and in tears.

"Bob, we've lost Chip Cobley!" was the only coherent thing he could say just as Joe drove up with the car.

"Get hold of yourself, Mike. Where is Chip?" I demanded.

"I don't know. The last I saw of him he was rolling over and over through that last rapid. The canoe's a total wreck. Got hung up in a root jam in that clump of trees. Some people had camped there. Maybe they saw him. That's just below where I swam ashore."

Without a word we drove on to the camp site where a man was trying to calm his wife. Out of the corner of one eye I caught a glimpse of the wrecked canoe temporarily held in the tangled mass of exposed roots that extended into the flooding river.

"You're sure in real trouble, Mac," the camper exclaimed as I skidded to a muddy stop. "We saw that poor boy rolling past here. Heaven only knows where he is by now!"

2

Backward-Flying Thunderbirds

Spinning the station wagon around, I forced the vehicle as fast as I dared over the rutty road. Fortunately every foot of the route paralleled the river with an unobstructed view of both banks. At length—three miles below the last ripple of Round Three—the boys pointed toward a wide sandy beach that jetted out from the right bank.

"Stop, Bob," yelled Little Wolf. "There's Chip!"

Sprawled out on his back, his head on his life jacket, lay the limp form of Chip Cobley. Missing were his hat, shirt, one shoe, and one pants leg. At the sound of the car horn he raised one arm. Rushing down to the bank, we shouted across the river for him to remain where he was. About half an hour of sunlight remained.

Driving back to the foot of Round Three where the other canoes were beached, I sent Milner, Krahulik, Laine, and Kem downstream to rescue Chip. Close, Shannon, and I returned to the bank opposite the sand bar to be ready to receive him if he was able to be lifted into a canoe and brought across the river. The boys paddled downstream faster than I could drive down the road. When we arrived, they were fighting the obstinate current for a left bank beaching. Imagine my relief when I saw Chip sitting on a center thwart! Kem and Laine were already sloughing their canoe up through the sage.

"How bad, Chip?" I asked as the boys rammed the bow into the gumbo bank.

"It's my back, just above my hips. I must have hit fifty rocks!"

One elbow was noticeably swollen and bleeding, both knees were black and blue, and a goose egg shone above his left temple. There was one encouraging sign: he walked quite normally. Plainly then, his most serious wound was invisible—a very brutally clobbered pride.

"We've let you down, Bob. It was more my fault than Kem's. We can't go on in just three canoes," Cobley hastened to add. Neither pretense nor vulgarity existed in Chip Cobley. He didn't curse his luck; he was above the manufacture of excuses.

"You've all got to discover that we don't indulge in any re-hash of blame when things go wrong," I assured them when we were all assembled. "There's a level bank down the road. We'll have to hurry to set up camp before dark and build mosquito fires. So let's drive back and get the other canoes."

The camper and his wife, delighted to see Chip alive, helped us extricate the twisted, caved-in craft from the watery tangle of roots.

"May as well leave it," I said after examining it. "Three hundred bucks down the drain! And no way to replace it."

"Aw, we can fix it," Kem assured me.

"Mike, be reasonable! Look at the keel seam—split from stem to stern. And the keel itself. They couldn't straighten that out at the factory. The bow's bent thirty degrees out of line and half the ribs are torn out by the roots. Look at

Canoe in which Chip Cobley and Mike Kem capsized in Round Three Rapid. We worked a full day hammering out the wrinkles and re-riveting seams.

---

the rents in both sides. This is the canoe the moose were kicking. It's jinxed! Let's junk it and go on in three canoes."

"Bob," Shannon said, "what it took a rock to do, it takes a rock to fix. By dropping big boulders onto the inside we can straighten her out. We have plenty of extra rivets, calking, and tools. It shouldn't take too long."

"All right," I said. "Tie her on the trailer and let's get the other one."

We were all bushed and depressed. A frigid wind drained off the snow-clad peaks and seemed to settle over our campsite. The boys kept bringing in squaw wood for the fire, so that by nine o'clock we were all dry once more. How different the outlook from warm bodies and full stomachs! Toga-ed in a blanket, Chip finally inched his way into the circle of firelight, and we all leaned back against our own private rocks for his account of what had happened.

"We hit the water too slowly to make the right channel. In current that fast there was nothing we could do to keep from ramming that dead tree. The water pulled like a hawser. Once we were back in the canoe, everything would have been more or less okay if it hadn't been for the rapid below Round Three. The rope on the paddle loom got wrapped around my leg, and when the canoe hit the first rock and rolled over, I let the paddle go but only got tangled up in the rope worse than ever. Then the canoe turned over again and stayed bottom up. I couldn't get out from under it on account of the rope around my leg. I nearly drowned. Must have swallowed a gallon of water! Kem got the canoe right side up just before we rammed another boulder. He whipped out his hunting knife when he saw I was tangled up in that rope and cut me loose. That saved my life. I pushed free from the canoe, but just then the current pulled me down one of those sluices and I went under again. One rock got me in the small of the back. The life jacket brought me to the surface and held my head out of the water while I tried to swim, but you can't swim in that stuff. I was facing upstream and couldn't even turn around. The current dragged my rear end over every boulder in the channel. One jagged rock ripped my shirt off and broke a strap on the life jacket. Some snag tore off the left pants leg and shoe at the same time. Thought I'd lost my whole leg. Everything went black and I quit fighting it. The next I knew, my feet were dragging along the bottom. I wasn't going so fast any more. There was a sandy beach and willows. I grabbed a branch and pulled myself ashore. I was so numb from the cold water I couldn't even feel the mosquitoes chewing my whole body. Then I heard the horn of the car."

"Old Mother Green teaches us her first lesson," said Little Wolf delightedly, admiring Chip's adventure.

From the camp we could hear the river's throaty rumble melding with the wails of coyotes, the calls of nighthawks, and the wind's whisper trickling through the sage. In Round Three we had asked for formal acquaintance with the river, and in her stony handshake we recognized her first lesson, a logical first lesson in the stern, unrelenting discipline she would demand of us for the full duration of her course.

"We *should* have made that rapid." Chip said.

"To quote Gibran: 'What can you do well the first time that will compare with the spider's first web or the oriole's first nest?' " I wasn't sure they got the message.

A coyote, losing a race through camp with a jack rabbit, scrambled the breakfast utensils and woke me up before dawn the next morning. Before I could talk myself out of the sleeping bag, Joe Krahulik was up kindling a fire. The smells of breakfast were usually alarm clock enough for everyone else, but it generally took a threat of the cold water treatment to separate Milner from his sleeping bag. After pancakes and sausage, we began the task of major surgery on the crippled Thunderbird. Prognosis: the scrap heap.

"Sorry, old girl," I heard Joe say as he brought out the tool box, "we'll have to operate without ether."

First, we drilled out the remaining rivets which held

the seats, thwarts, and ribs. As Mike Shannon had suggested, we dropped heavy boulders inside the hull to straighten out the keel which was a long V-shaped member riveted to the bottom from bow-to-stern bangstrips. Dozens of the keel's rivets had been shorn off or ripped out during the ordeal of the day before. In order to avoid side distortion as we straightened the keel six inches at a session, we were forced to hammer out the hull at the same time. The alloy had the spring and resistance of steel without the resilience of steel, but perseverance finally overcame the metal's built-in stubbornness. The sides were reshaped before filling the open rents with Epoxy cement and hammering the gashes closed. For anvils we used head-size, glacier-polished monoliths of quartz. Most difficult to remodel were the gunnels which, before the crack-up, had been machine-rounded hollow tubes. Except for the keel, the gunnels had taken the worst beating in the rapids.

By five o'clock that afternoon all re-riveting was completed; thwarts, seats, and ribs were back in place; the keel seam was re-calked with aluminum cement; and most of the dents were hammered out of the hull. When all her wounds had been dressed, the boys set the canoe on the water to check for leaks. She was tight and ready to roll—but not like new.

Between Round Three and the village of Daniel the Green River flowed out of the hills and meandered through open sage moors and grassy meadows. One long series of fast water rapids was troublesome enough but negotiable, thanks to this period of high water that floated us over boulders which, during normal flow, would have been exposed. Barbed-wire drift fences made the otherwise smooth run hazardous. We soon learned to paddle a course as close to the bank as possible for short-notice stops. Pursuing any other course, due to the speed and stubborn strength of the current, we would have been hurled into the barbed wire before we could beach. The bow of the canoe would go under the bottom strand, but you can imagine what the barbs could have done to the belly and chest of the bowman in his sitting position. "A do-it-your-self hara-kiri kit": Mike Laine's metaphor was an all-day sucker for thought, and he didn't have to invent any audience to appreciate the possibilities his remark suggested.

Above a right angle bend of the river, not far upstream from Daniel, stood the propped remains of old Fort Bonneville, built about 1832. The Mountain Men—Smith, Jackson, Sublette of the famous Rocky Mountain Fur Company—held their rendezvous at this site before and after the heyday of the fort. In 1835, during one such wild and woolly get-together known as the notorious Green River Rendezvous, the revelry among the trappers and Indians attained such bacchanalian proportions that the U.S. Army temporarily withdrew.

At Daniel we unloaded at the Green River bridge and parked the station wagon and trailer behind Blackman's garage. Food boxes, duffle, cooking gear, and the thousand and one odds and ends had to be equally divided and loads balanced. For fear of the day when a total loss might occur, we never placed all of any one indispensable, such as repair kits, vital utensils, or first aid supplies, in a single canoe. Each craft would float filled with water and two boys aboard, but not filled with water, two boys, and five hundred pounds of food and dunnage. Each canoe carried two extra paddles and two fifty-foot painters of half-inch nylon.

One mile east of Daniel, above the left bank of the Green, was the site of Father Pierre Jean De Smet's *La Prairie de la Messe*, where, on July 5, 1840, Wyoming's first Holy Mass was celebrated. Father De Smet certainly occupies a top-rung position among famous early western pioneers, and the legend of his life (1801–1873) has been the subject of innumerable publications. His influence and memory are still very much alive today in Wyoming. One of the good padre's favorite yarns made himself the brunt of a stroke of irony. In 1835, the Reverend Samuel Parker, a Protestant minister, preached the first Christian sermon in the Rocky Mountains at Bondurant, Wyoming, about thirty miles from Daniel: thus, according to De Smet, "the Presbyterians beat the Jesuits to the draw with Satan by almost five years!"

Below Daniel, the riparian growth of willows, cotton-woods, alders, box elders, and hawthorns grew as a densely matted jungle. The snow-capped Wind River Mountains dominated the eastern horizon and sent down a roaring tributary every mile or so. The plainlike valley and shriveled hills between the Wind River to the east and the far-spread Gros Ventres to the west applied the brakes to the Green's wild roll and forced the stream to break up into several beds. The gently rising prairie above the low banks provided fattening summer pasturage for thousands of head of cattle, sheep, and horses.

Reading the river from the lead canoe, Milner and I rounded one of the frequent meanders and saw a barbed-wire drift fence dead ahead. Blowing the whistle for attention, I shouted, "Prepare to beach behind me, left bank."

Reese and I seized some exposed roots that hung down the five-foot perpendicular mudbank and began jockeying our way downstream, ready to lift the wire so the others could get under. Mike Laine and Little Wolf came alongside, making it virtually impossible for Milner and I to complete the maneuver. Shannon and Krahulik beached about fifty yards upstream, much too far away to be of any help should an emergency arise. Kem and Cobley decided to "sky-hook" some overhanging branches of gooseberry whose thorns they failed to observe.

In the painful confusion that followed, the pair capsized in four feet of rushing ice water. Those of us nearby dove into the stream to rescue sleeping bags, duffle, fishing rods, and tarps. When Mike finally righted the canoe and removed some of the thorns from his hand, he began screaming orders and accusations at Cobley, who ignored him and calmly went about repacking, much like a Great Dane scorning the snarls of a Chihuahua.

"One of these days you'll get your chance to paddle the River Styx, Kem, if you don't start using your head for thinking," Reese warned. Milner and I were irked that the boys had delayed the relay of the command and had reacted so slowly, yet the incident provided a valuable lesson which the boys remembered for the rest of the trip.

Five miles below Daniel, a long, clifflike peninsula called Mesa Point extended down from the foothills of the Gros Ventres to the very right bank of the Green. At this headland all channels converged and, except for islands, the river bed never divided again for over 2000 miles. Beyond the conflux of all the channels, the stream picked up speed. The color, for which the Green may well have been named, was now an even pea green; the banks were low and terraced, forested with luxuriant cottonwoods and box elders. Beds of goldenrod and sunflowers blossomed

34 df

along the terraces and between the trees as if they had been planted and cultivated. Open hills were ablaze with flame-colored prickly-pear cactus flowers.

Well-drilled squads of mustang horses bolted from the groves and followed their sergeants into the hills where they observed us from what they considered a safer distance. Moose slopped around in every bog; otters got their kicks out of heckling ill-tempered beavers in the backwater pools; grazing deer, elk, and antelope snubbed scattered herds of white-faced Herefords and acres of domestic sheep. Flocks of ducks, geese, and heron rose before us, then circled back to their open-air markets after we had passed. Coveys of quail, partridge, pheasant, and sage hen held excited conferences at the sight of the four strange monsters in the middle of their river. Chip's solemn warning to the other boys was: "Leave everything alone that birds build!"

Contentious Old Mother Green never allowed us the luxury to fully daydream through the ever-changing pageant along her shores. She constantly prodded our attention to log jams, gravel bars, islands, whirlpools, barbed-wire drift fences, and minor rapids. Beyond the De Smet parish, the limits of whose jurisdiction depended upon how far the intrepid priest could ride to minister to a sick Indian or to rescue a stranded Oregon-bound wagon train, the river threw up a series of tests.

Shortly before Boulder Creek splashed into the Green, the great river bent back toward the southeast as if for a final farewell nod to her maternal Wind River glaciers. A feisty little wind had sneaked in from behind, and we weren't paying too much attention to it. Actually the gentle stern gusts soon eliminated any need for paddling beyond steering. The sensation was fun. But a downstream wind also sweeps before it all warning sounds of approaching events.

I was listening to summer cicadas whistling their fragile tunes and watching the journeys of floating seeds when, without a whisper of announcement, we were eased around a wooded bend and instantly catapulted into a long, raging rapid. Five hundred yards downstream, a big bushy island complicated the problem by splitting the channel. Half way through the choppy course the wind shifted, snatched us all by the necks, shook us until our teeth rattled, and threw gallons of icy spray into our faces.

Blowing the whistle I always wore around my neck, I shouted: "Right channel! Prepare to beach!" I chose the right channel for no other reason than the fact that we found ourselves being thrown to the right of the center of the rapid. The wind garbled my command and the boys misinterpreted it: "Sight animal! Bear on the beach!"

Oddly enough, no sooner were the words out of my mouth than an enormous black bruin crashed out of the underbrush and stood upright at the edge of the water on the only beach where we could possibly have gotten ashore. I wasn't about to contest his superior weight, claws, and molars.

"Rock! Left, Bob! Left!" thundered Reese, and I switched paddling sides, dug in until it felt as if someone had thrust a stiletto between my shoulder blades, and missed the barely submerged boulder by an uncomfortable two-inch margin.

I heard the boys in the following canoes relaying the same command as each alert bowman sighted the menace.

Although we had agreed that no one would talk during the running of a rapid, other than to relay commands, Mike Laine always violated the pact with cheers and guffaws every time Old Mother Green kicked the bottom of his Leaping Thunderbird.

Downstream from the last throes of the rapid was 1000 yards of warm, roomy, sandy beach—no deerflies, no mosquitoes, not a breath of wind.

"Prepare to beach," I ordered.

"Hey, Bob," Mike Shannon said when we were ashore, "we shipped a lot of water back there. Why didn't you stop and read it?"

"I chose to get drenched because this is such a nice beach to dry out on!" I retorted.

After spreading the wet gear on the sand, we had tuna and crackers, chocolate bars, and Jell-O drink. While we were stretched out on the warm beach for a siesta, the notion kept recurring to me that we were being watched. I finally sat up and rubbernecked around but couldn't pinpoint any specific interloper. Dozens of birds sat around on branches and stared; the fact that they had stopped singing further alerted me. I hadn't dismissed that bear. Unable to resist curiosity any longer, I got up to inspect the shrubbery beneath the cottonwoods.

In the center of a clearing about fifty yards from the beach stood a gentle-appearing mature coyote. As I approached, he neither growled nor retreated. In order that he might observe all my movements, I stepped slowly into the clearing and sat down. He backed up several steps, sniffed the air, then relaxed on his haunches without turning his twinkling yellow eyes away for a second. He dis-

Pause for lunch. It was here the coyote sneaked in and stole Reese Milner's candy bar. Mike Shannon, Chip Cobley, Mike Kem, and Craig Close prepare to push on.

played neither hostility nor fear, just a friendly interest and a sort of expression of delight in finding that something was going on.

"If I could only converse in the language of your world, old fellow, I'd tell you what a fine citizen I really think you are. You've been vilified long enough."

He had just turned his head to one side as if trying to comprehend when, in an explosive flash of flying dead leaves and a shower of sand, my new friend's mate, something gripped between her teeth, rushed across the clearing from the direction of the beach. Together, the two coyotes trotted over the hill behind the cottonwoods.

"Hey!" I heard Milner shout a moment later, "which one of you bums stole my candy bar?"

That afternoon a southwest wind got up and quartered our bows. Periodic gusts blew with such force that the surface of the river appeared to flow back upstream. Dig as we did, we could make no headway against the blasts that chopped up dangerous whitecaps which in their turn sent columns of big, hemispherical bubbles back up the river. We wanted no part of a long tangle of islands, log jams, and snags in that wind, so, between gusts, we raced to the lee side of a wooded island and waited. Fluffy, low-hanging nimbus clouds moved overhead with surprising speed.

During periods of relative calm we paddled as fast as we could to make up for lost time. At length we entered a region of abandoned log cabins, homes of early settlers who had liked the valley of the Green, who had farmed the flatlands, but who had raised no second generation to remain there. Before the settlers, the lusty Mountain Men of beaver-trapping days in the 1820s and 1830s considered the valley an ideal place to spend the forty-below-zero winters with their Shoshone squaws. The few remaining walls of their rock cabins could be plainly seen from the river. We explored several such sites for souvenirs, but one hundred and fifty years of Wyoming weather had left very little in the way of artifacts. We picked up arrowheads around the scattered ruins of former army forts, grim re-minders of unsung gallantry on both sides during the bloody cavalry-Indian battles.

At four o'clock the wind became impossible. One gust on an open stretch caught the insides of the canoes, spun them momentarily, and sent us back upstream. We had little more than turned around when a steady squall took hold of us again and pushed all four craft backward no matter how hard we paddled.

"Backward flying Thunderbirds!" Kem shouted, coughing. "This wind blows even my words right back down my throat!"

"Ha!" Reese grabbed the opportunity—I knew someone would—"and crams them right back down where they belong!"

The most we could do was sit in the middle of the stream and balance the canoes to keep from turning over. A passing flock of ravens, hitting the wall of weather, were literally somersaulted out of the air and toppled into the groaning cottonwoods. We watched a golden eagle accept the challenge by flying into a thermal updraft. When he opened his wings for a soar, he lost a shower of feathers and was pushed backward through the air, just as the canoes were reversed on the river.

For half an hour we kept up the unequal struggle and continued to lose ground. Eventually we were able to back into the rocks of a left bank beach and tie up. By five o'clock we began to worry about locating a campsite. Comfortable places to spend the night were rare along the Green and had to be pre-empted when they appeared, regardless of the hour.

Although we were all using pomade against the sun and wind, I noticed several pairs of cracked and bleeding lips. Mike Shannon's formerly lily-white cheeks were checkered with scabby scales like the belly of a baby alligator. We were all nursing paddling blisters.

"What time is it?" Mike Laine asked absentmindedly.

"Who cares?" was the concerted answer from the three who had canoed with me in Canada.

"Bob never allows any form of time machine on a wilderness trip," Joe explained. "Says it's like eating ice cream topped with mustard."

The sun was still about an hour above the Gros Ventres when the wind finally allowed us to proceed to an open grassy shelf where we spent a reasonably comfortable night.

The smell of smoke awakened me in time to enjoy a spectacular sunrise behind Joe Krahulik's thawing fire. Heavy dew of the evening before had frozen into frost during the night, and the outside covers of the sleeping bags were crystalline and white. Yet thirty minutes after sunrise, the frost had melted back into dew again.

Camp duties on this trip were not assigned; they were understood. Each person assumed responsibility for what he wanted to be his exclusive domain—not out of selfishness or distaste for another chore but out of recognition of a need and of his ability to dispatch it. The system didn't always work out, but intelligent discussion, rather than dictation, resolved what many campers regard as the bane of camping. The universally distasteful job of scouring pots and pans shifted daily.

Before we could finish a quick breakfast of Tang, gluey oatmeal, fried ham, and cocoa, the deerflies, blackflies, gnats, no-see-ums, and mosquitoes had dined well on our blood supplies, despite generous applications of several popular "guaranteed" brands of repellents. Long ago I arrived at the conclusion that the old Hudson's Bay formula—pennyroyal, citronella, and bergamot dissolved in petroleum jelly—was the only effective repellent. But the conviction always brought up the question: Which was worse, the insects or the smell of the horrid formula?

The river continued to break around the prows of countless islands. The current was fast and clear. By noon we were cruising beside high, pink cliffs through which the river had carved prodigious amphitheaters. The general tone of the landscape became barren, with less evidence that early settlers had found it to their liking. Rapids occurred with greater frequency but proved mild, due to the deep water of heavy run off from the Rockies: it was shallow water that produced the headaches. Gradually the river nosed into a land of distant mesas, buttes, and broken plateaus. We didn't call it a desert because the entire summer surface flourished with rippling wild rye, stipa, wheatgrass, and the international shepherd's purse. Sarape-like bands of wild flowers followed the contours of the hills and buttes for as far as we could see.

Moose, deer, elk, and otter were still plentiful, while colonies of great blue heron, which had turned entire cottonwood groves into apartment houses *à la belle étoile*, coughed their indignation at our momentary intrusion upon their privacy. It was not uncommon to observe heron and sandhill cranes nesting in the same dead cottonwood along with bald eagles and redtail hawks. A law of the wild had established a peace treaty during nesting. I counted fourteen masterpieces of oriole architecture on one branch. Stilted killdeer, terns, sandpipers, and petrels patrolled both banks of the river to beat the ducks and geese to the wriggling food supply.

A southwest wind prevailed and miles-high thunderstorm fronts piled up around the disappearing Wind River and Gros Ventres peaks now far to the north behind us. By early afternoon we experienced a repetition of the day before—though we paddled our hearts out, the Leaping Thunderbirds planed backward upstream while boiling little wakes from our bows went the other way.

As the valley of the Green slowly began to narrow between high-pitched cliffs of pink Wasatch clays, the river admitted the Piney complex of creeks from the southern Gros Ventres foothills, the last perennially running tributaries in the state of Wyoming. The channel deepened, islands disappeared altogether, a perceptible cargo of silt altered the Green's taste and color, and the river moderated her mad rush after the last Piney tributary joined the 10,000 cubic feet per second flood.

Exhausted by the long day and the struggle with the wind, we were beaching at what appeared to be an ideal campsite near an open "sink" when Joe Krahulik jumped out onto a gray surface of wet sand which bore hundreds of clear prints of ducks and geese. The weight of his body drove his left leg into the muck up to his thigh. Unable to withdraw, he lost his balance and fell forward. The entire flat shook like a bowl of thin jelly, the birds' footprints disappeared, a film of water rose to the surface at the same instant, and the unstable earth carried ripples of mercury-like shock waves which gulped at our struggling companion.

"Quicksand!" I shouted. "Throw him a rope!"

"It's okay, Bob," Joe said quietly. "I can reach the canoe." Joe had the faculties of a general: instant recognition of the most orderly sequences in any emergency.

"Don't anybody get out!" I warned.

Joe quickly reached for the port gunnel of his canoe. He

had sunk almost to his chest. Laboriously he pulled himself up from the sucking ooze that gobbled at his legs, while the boys in the boat alongside held down the starboard gunnel of his canoe. Even when bogged down in quicksand, Joe's disciplined muscles moved with the shrewd timing of a panther.

Having marshaled all our remaining strength to refloat the four mired craft, we then did no more than "sit" our rigging without paddling until a rocky shore with a campsite appeared two miles below the quicksand swamp.

With camp set up high and dry in a sheltered grove of alders, everyone fell onto his sleeping bag and relaxed until dusk. After recording the day's events in his diary, Close walked to the beach for two pails of water. On the way back to camp he stopped, turned, ground his teeth, squinted at the swirling river, and spat out: "Bandit!"

Heading for a bath, Joe overheard the insult. "Think of her as a one-lane highway, Little Wolf," he said, "a big one-way road to adventure you can't get any other way."

3

A School
for Decoys

I started the breakfast fire even before dawn began to kindle a southeastern horizon of clouds. An upstream breeze brought in the delicious fragrance of rain and dewy marshes, while birds and other choruses of little voices awoke earlier than usual that morning.

We began the day's paddling four abreast down a narrowing channel where bloated floods had chopped their way through a squat community of identical, weary-looking hills. In order that we might appreciate the magnitude of her handicraft, the Green had planted no bankside screen of trees or shrubbery of any kind. The savage rumbadoon of distant tom-toms soon announced the proximity of new reading material. The boys dropped back into single file as the hoarse wind, sounding as if it had the sniffles that morning, stuttered and lisped Old Mother Green's liquid message. Easing along on surface current, we helmed as closely as possible to the shore. From a concealing bend under a right-bank arcade of overhanging cliffs came the unmistakable bass of a major rapid.

"Close parallel with the beach!" I called when the crests hove into view.

Having belayed the aft painters around shoreline rocks

in order to keep the bows downstream, we hiked along the
left bank for a careful reading of the river's instructions.
The rapid, four hundred yards long and wicked every jump
of the way, gnawed viciously at the undercut cliffs along
the right bank. The narrowing channel endeavored to ac-
commodate both the full volume of the stream and a bed
of boulders. The waves piled up on each other and splashed
both banks.

"Better toss in a log and run it through to test her
throw," Reese advocated, remembering our experiences
with some rough water in Canada.

But when we brought up a deadfall and nosed it through
the first crests, it turned abruptly and slammed head-on like
a torpedo into the cliff. As the current carried it downstream, the missile was drawn momentarily away from the
wall only to give it speed for the next collision. By actual
count, the log crashed into the solid rock bank fifteen times
before it reached the end of the semi-circular course
around the cliff. The same would happen to a canoe, except
no canoe ever built could endure fifteen slams against that
wall. Along the left bank the river deployed dozens of
boulders in the correct order to make canoeing impossible.
Thus, the only practical course lay along the white water,
slightly to the left of the midstream crests.

"We better rope it, Bob," Mike Kem suggested.

"Just like trying to ride a porpoise," Mike Shannon
declared.

"She's like a mustang that ain't been broke," drawled a
strange voice from the overhead bank behind us. "To
halter's one thing; to ride, another."

We whirled around to find we had an audience of one
hundred head of Herefords and two double-jawed pokes on

chestnut Morgan quarters. The roar of the rapid and the canyon updraft had muffled their approach.

"You'll croak if you try to shoot them rapids," warned the second cowhand. He sat with one leg draped around his saddle horn, rolling a Bull Durham cigarette with the thumb and forefinger of one hand.

"I'd rather meet a vinegarone," his companion asserted. "You couldn't get me in that river on the *Queen Mary!* See that wrecked skiff down yonder at the other end?" We had noticed the battered vessel from a distance. "Sheriff's still lookin' for the bodies."

Wyoming cowboys have always generated and maintained their own special breed of Americans. Hard-bitten, hard-boiled, hard-singing devotees of rustic reality and prairie bel canto, they sing what they can't say; and when they do say it, they generally exhale their own idioms with compound interest. Their big unpeopled miles are wider, longer miles; and the saddle horse is still important in their everyday lives. These people are the direct descendants of an eager generation of pioneers, those with the guts to stay and wrest a living from a hostile land. Their traditions are raw and basic, uncomplicated by nervous disorders, stomach ulcers, and allergies. Their land extends beyond their bony, local horizons, and, like their land, their love for their fellow men and for their country extends far beyond any personal horizon.

After an exchange of amenities, the non-smoking cowhand said, "You doin' this river by canoe?"

"We're trying to be the first ones ever to canoe the Green," Chip volunteered.

"And if you make the wrong move?" the older man asked with a cynical smile.

"Curtains!" Milner answered with finality.

"Think it'll rain today?" Mike Laine asked.

"Don't know. Folks out here won't discuss the weather. It's always obvious."

Convinced we could run the rapid with less risk than stringing the canoes along the shoreline with ropes, I asked the boys to come down one at a time on strictest formula. The cowboys agreed to hold back their thirsty herd until we had passed.

"You've got a rough row to hoe, boys," one called in farewell. "Don't get caught in the furrow!"

"And watch out for vinegarones and milermore birds," yelled the other.

The Leaping Thunderbirds rode the backs of the white-maned cataract with greater ease than I had anticipated. Although carrying normal loads, they ricocheted from crest to crest like Ping-Pong balls, but somehow the river kept us off the froth-girded rocks which had appeared so ominous from the beach. Beaching beyond the whirlpools, we used our drinking cups to bail out what water we had shipped.

"That was great! Let's unload, take the canoes back there below the cattle, and run it again," Mike Kem begged.

"Kem, you've swamped so many times, your mind's waterlogged," Milner taunted. "Didn't I hear you begging to string this one?"

Wedged between two boulders at the end of the rapid and weighted down by plaited driftwood were the rotting timbers of the dead skiff hanging slightly above the present water level as a riverside exhibit of the stream's potential craftsmanship in disaster.

"Why is it the deepest cuts are always on the right bank?" I heard Kem ask Cobley.

"Ferrel's Law," Chip said, remembering his physics. "Bodies in motion in the northern hemisphere have a tendency to swerve to the right due to the earth's rotation. So the deepest erosion is on right-bank bends."

In beaver ponds where the water was still, we observed all the driftwood on the right side of the pool. The highest bluffs had been cut on the right bank, and where there was evidence of a flood plain, the river generally flowed on the right side of the plain. The phenomenon is most easily demonstrated along the route of a north-to-south flowing river like the Green. The amphitheater-like cliffs proved it.

To understate it, there has always been so much to learn and relearn on every wilderness river. To the canoeist, each stream remains eternally new. Introducing young people to our rivers should be a part of our national heritage. I've never known a river to graduate a bum.

We had seen enough of Old Mother Green up to this point to realize we could never fathom all her hidden meanings and rhythmic epic. At first we begrudged her that ancient wisdom, an indelible language we saw scrawled across her 15 million-year-old trough. She must have known for ages what she would require of two-legged creatures attempting to paddle through her crests; that was why she occasionally cast our canoes on the rocks, then taught us to forge our own tools to reshape the wreckage. By now we had collided with several of her moments of truth. We had seen the extermination she had to offer those who defied or ignored her disciplines. We saw her munching at the wrecks along her shorelines to punctuate her points. The education she offered was a minute-by-minute, mile-by-mile prodding of thought and initiative—Old Mother Nature's way.

Below what we called Dead Skiff Rapid, the river widened, and as the shoreline seemed to float by, I became aware of mumbling from the other canoes. The boys paddled up alongside.

"Hey, Bob, what's a vinegarone?" It was a collective question.

"Horrible creatures," I explained. "Direct descendants of the Desert Makers. If one ever gets in your sleeping bag, brother, you've had it! That's why you saw those cowboys wearing firearms."

"Strange you never mentioned them before—or milermore birds, either," Joe Krahulik contended, his downy chin thrust forward to keep from cracking up. "Just what *are* milermore birds?"

"They're big old country birds that come in assorted colors and sizes. I'll point out the next one I see."

The boys jeered a little and dropped back to mull over the two unknown creatures; they nourished no hankering to be taken on any Wyoming version of a snipe hunt.

Paddling somewhat closer together than good judgment dictated, we were about half way down a narrow channel to the right of an island when the current began to boil up from the river bed and pelt the canoe bottoms with gravel. Under the rasping shock of surprise we failed to note that the current had reversed on the side closest to the island. Suddenly the river seized all four bows, threw the canoes broadside, and slammed them into one another for a compound collision. Laine and Shannon were hurled into the river. I wanted to beach at once, but one look at the texture of either shore reminded me of poorly cooked oatmeal. Obviously quicksand.

In a sculling maneuver, Little Wolf picked up Shannon, while Krahulik sterned the ornery repaired canoe up alongside his bowman for a rescue. Fifty yards back upstream, the reversed current became absorbed and we resumed our way. Each boy had met his own responsibility in the emergency without any help or advice from me. Very often I helped them most by interfering the least.

"How long is this river going to continue this absurd hostility?" Shannon demanded when he was once again in a paddling position.

Reese looked back, and I braced myself for the shot I knew he was about to fire. "For just so long as you two mental midgets neglect to wear your life jackets." Since the lesson was self-apparent, I throttled the urge to make a speech.

It might have been simpler to have delegated all the thinking to one committee and let the rest do all the work, but under such leadership, I'm sure the trip would have belonged exclusively to the thinkers, while dull and unhappy memories would have haunted everyone else. From the very beginning, these boys recognized the principle that no one played an accessory role out here; it was a united effort and no member was more important than another.

Below the next island we observed a dark spot in the center of the river where the split channel compressed itself back into one deep bed.

"What do you make of that, Bob?" Reese asked.

Within a nick of time I recognized the dark well as a "death-hole" whirlpool. By paddling as fast as possible, we earned the necessary speed to miss the well and overcome the down-funneling water at the narrowing lip.

"*Mamma mia!*" Reese exclaimed. One side glance down the fourteen-inch hole revealed a spinning ten-foot log twenty feet below. The strength and speed of the current in the stationary whirlpool had been sufficient to trap the log and hold it in one position.

A good fast river can teach acute observation as nothing else can, yet there were certain observable values along the Green which I found very difficult to impart to the boys. For instance, they saw distant drift dunes but failed to appreciate the colors of changing lights and shadows on the sand. They often cast a photographically fast glance at a sunset but missed the westward flight of a homing dove or the evening song of the ouzel. When we passed through an atmosphere charged with the fragrance of datura, lupine, or evening primrose, Mike Laine would comment: "Stinks like that stuff my mom puts on when she drags my old man out to an opera!"

On the debit side of the ledger, however, the boys were quickly inclined toward an eagerness to cooperate with our wild associates along the route. I was delighted when they began to avoid stepping on flowers, and no furry, feathery, or scaly creature ever left our camp hungry—even when our rations were skimpy.

It was about noon when we beached at the village of La Barge. While the boys were admiring the malts and hamburgers in the local café, I was in the market refilling the food boxes for the final ninety-mile run into the city of Green River.

That afternoon we paddled down an almost continuous

series of stormy rapids, backwaters, and whirlpools, to a wide shallow which we recognized as the site of the old Mormon Ferry. During periods of low water, the Green's gravel bed was fordable at this bend by wagons and stage-coaches on their way to California, Utah, and Oregon. Even after a century of disuse the old wagon-wheel ruts are still plainly visible, coming down the gulches from the east and going out toward the sunset. Such routes as the Oregon Trail, the Mormon Trail, the California Trail, the Emigrant Trail, the Overland Stage Route, the Pony Express, and the Sublette Cut-Off (an older trail) —all converged to take advantage of the shallow crossing.

The boys beached to read the mid-nineteenth century messages carved on the sandstone face of Names Hill where hastily scrawled notices proclaimed tragedy and urgency for following friends and relatives. Names of many well-known pioneers and early pathfinders have been defaced by vandals carving their own initials into the wall. As

---

The site of the Mormon Ferry near La Barge, Wyoming. Most covered wagons of pioneer days crossed the Green River at this location because of the shallow, gravel bottom.

Crumbling remains of Overland Stage Coach and Pony Express Station. At this point Buffalo Bill Cody used to swim his horse across the Green when he was a Pony Express rider. Craig Close, fore; Mike Kem, aft.

a result of the irreparable damage they saw, the boys resolved to carve their initials nowhere on this trip. That night we camped in a ravine where relics of pioneer days lay rusting away, where many a mother had abandoned household treasures to lighten the wagon load for the climb ahead.

In the course of the twelve miles between Emigrant Ford and the Seedskadee Lake, we saw moose, converging flocks of thousands of geese and ducks, as well as the usual beaver colonies. On one occasion, Little Wolf pointed out an entire hillside on the move, a typically fast-grazing herd of pronghorn antelope.

By one o'clock we had paddled the ten-mile length of

Seedskadee Lake to within a few yards of the newly constructed Fontenelle Dam. We carried the canoes and their
contents to the side of the abandoned little road where we
awaited Mr. and Mrs. Cleo Brown. We had met in La
Barge, and they had volunteered to haul us and our equipment by truck around the dam. My precision thermometer
registered 120 degrees Fahrenheit, and the only shade was
the flimsy shadow cast by the sparse and sultry sage which
grew to a maximum height of fourteen inches. Propping up
the canoes with food boxes, we erected shade in which to
sit and wilt at 110 degrees.

When Jedediah Strong Smith (1798–1831), most famous of all Great Basin explorers and pathfinders, first
paddled an Indian pirogue down this section of the Green,
he named the river the Seedskadee after the Crow Indian
word for prairie chicken. The name has all but disappeared,
but thousands of the birds still call these hills home, so the
government has perpetuated Smith's colorful nomenclature in the big federal water project known as Seedskadee
Lake.

Each early voyageur of beaver-trapping days saw his
opportunity to stamp his mark upon a rapidly unfolding
story by naming the river. William P. Hunt, commander of
the Astoria Overland Expedition (1811–1812) seven years
after the Lewis and Clark Expedition, was probably the
first white man ever to lay eyes on this section of the Green
River, which—to his eternal credit—he neglected to name.
Regardless of the number of christenings Old Mother
Green has undergone, priority must logically be directed to
Hernando de Alarcón and García López de Cárdenas who,
in 1540, discovered Labyrinth Canyon above the conflu-

ence of the Green and the Colorado, and referred to the stream as *El Río Verde de la Buena Guía:* "The Green River of Good Guidance."

Before the arrival of the Browns and the truck, huge thunderheads had crowded in above. By the time our equipment was loaded, the storm hit with a Wyoming peak of fury. The wind came in sixty-mile-an-hour gusts and the rain turned into pea-size hail which pelted us throughout the ride to the other side of the dam.

Madder than a pinched hornet at her temporary confinement behind the great earth-filled structure, Old Mother Green came snorting out into space from two center flumes at the base of the dam. For three miles below the site she bucked and kicked like a liberated mustang in a cocklebur patch. To give full vent to her rage, she drafted the wind, and the two lurching forces churned the channel into a convulsion that no canoe could withstand.

An early camp is always a good camp. The extra time now permitted us the luxury of a rock-lined pit for a fireplace which became a refuse pit when we buried it the next morning before leaving. Over the coals we cooked our regular meal and afterward sat around baking "long-tailed pies"—jam rolled in thin Bisquick dough—twisted around peeled willow sticks and turned over the coals until crusty brown. The pit was also useful for roasting in aluminum foil and for baking corn dodgers or oatmeal pones.

The boys managed to eat their way through those six food boxes at the rate of 4500 calories each per day. Despite harvests of fish, acres of bushes that advertised ripe berries, salads of fern fiddlenecks and watercress, mustard and dandelion greens, most of our money went into groceries. Always with us was the unimaginative variety of canned meats which we disguised with dehydrated potatoes, cheese, onions, and chili powder. Of all foods, we considered such products as evaporated milk, corn, and dried fruit the most valuable for stoking furnaces that burned at the rate of four hundred calories per working hour.

Relaxation from the high-tension pitches of the river day was a necessity after camp was established. We engaged in activities designed to change the subject as well as to rest the hands, shoulders, feet, and neck muscles: a bird walk, an animal survey, a long slow hike through the hills in search of gem stones, petrified wood, fossils or arrowheads, a mountain climb, a photography lesson, a nap in the sun, a bull session, the daily diary entry.

The day following the Fontenelle Dam portage might well have been entitled the "Merry-Go-Round," so numerous were the whirlpools and backwater eddies which threw the Leaping Thunderbirds into a spin or two every time we tried to paddle across one. Among all the little unknowables that kept forever popping up, was the river's concerted attempt between the Fontenelle Dam and Slate Creek to violate Playfair's Principle (1822): that a mature stream neither erodes nor deposits silt, but lengthens its course through oxbows and meanders. Attempts by the river to violate the principle were to become very important in Utah.

Early in her beginnings as the centuries ticked slowly away, the region had been denuded of that pattern of important upper tributaries which typifies most of the great rivers of the world, robbed by the secondary dikes and rises along an ever-changing Continental Divide which rerouted the courses of such major potential contributors as the Gros Ventre, the Snake, and the Wind. Above the confluence with the Colorado, such questionable streams as the San Rafael, the Yampa, and the Uintah must be considered as minor feeders. The Green River's loss of water during one summer day by evaporation exceeds the combined contributions of every trunk stream between the Big Sandy and the Colorado during the same day, a distance flow of seven hundred miles!

During a rest stop I sat watching a bullfrog that issued a grateful croak every time he gulped a gnat. The sun's torrid rays bounced from the unshadowed brow of a former channel cliff and further irritated, even through dark glasses, the boys' partial sun blindness. The frog ignored the heat to devour the swarming insects. A tranquil downstream flight of a great blue heron, rowing through the heavy, drowsy air, was in sharp contrast with a flock of Canada geese engaged in a peculiar ritual along the shoreline farther down the river.

"The heat must have gotten to them," Mike Kem suggested with a chuckle.

The older ganders, like drill sergeants, kept herding the half-growns off the beach and into the water and back onto the beach again. A small flock of widgeons, sitting on the sideline, seemed to be giggling at the clumsy geese.

"They're drilling an awkward squad," Joe assured us. "My guess is they'll maneuver when they take off." Surely enough, when we flushed the flock, the corporals flew around in wide arcs and nudged the younger geese into a less ragged V.

When camp was established that afternoon, we walked down the high parapet to observe another flock of geese drilling the young on a midstream island.

When we stopped on the bank opposite the geese, the decoys went into action to warn the flock of our presence. A "decoy" is a goose—male or female—without a mate. Since the species mates but once during a lifetime, should either die, the survivor goes to school to learn to be a flock decoy in order to maintain his or her usefulness.

If a flock is in flight, the birds won't come down for a landing until the decoys have gone in and tested the area for hunters or predators. Due to their weight, the hardest thing for geese to do is become airborne. When they have to take off in a hurry, one or two geese remain behind gasping, feinting as cripples or slowpokes, thus attracting and holding the attention of the interloper until the flock is airborne. Geese are very loyal to their pattern leaders and, in the event of predator attack, a decoy will lead off to conceal the identity of the real leader. A flock will panic if anything happens to the leader.

The life of the decoy is in constant danger. Mortality rate is high because these birds willingly sacrifice their lives on a moment's notice, if necessary, to save the mated and younger members. In most flocks we saw individuals following and imitating the older decoys. These were student decoys learning all the tricks used in deceiving an enemy. Most decoys are lost during moulting because geese can't fly during that season. We concluded that the goose was the true aristocrat of river society.

The morning of July twenty-fourth broke clear and cooler. Everyone felt new vigor. With neither wind nor rapids, we experienced the happiest canoeing until we reached the mouth of Big Sandy Creek. This tributary had brought in a torrent of silty alkaline water and revolving mica flakes, washed down during recent cloudbursts in the Rocky Mountains near South Pass. As the river swung in and out among the Badland Hills, she gained speed. Massive carved cliffs of the colorful Zionlike Wasatch formation reappeared, higher, more ruggedly dissected, and all but barren of plant life. Behind us now were the green hill sarapes and flowering mesas; before us lay an unbroken horizon of smoldering desert where the color green existed only as copper rust between certain calcareous strata.

At five o'clock on the afternoon of that day we beached near the John Wesley Powell monument on Expedition Island, a large and beautifully landscaped public park within the city limits of Green River, Wyoming.

4

In Powell's Wake

The sheriff and a committee of citizens met us shortly after a difficult beaching—difficult because of precipitous banks along the island where no provision had been made for the mooring of boats. In fact, it was against the law to beach there. The officials displayed typically generous Green River hospitality by allowing us to camp in the park on the very spot where the intrepid Major John Wesley Powell camped at the beginning of his historic journey ninety-five years before. To a river man, this was hallowed ground. The eagle-eyed sheriff and his men questioned the boys and fine tooth combed our canoes and equipment to ascertain their condition and safety before allowing us to proceed.

"Looks as if you might make it," was the sheriff's succinct remark.

That night I treated the boys to a civilized café meal as a reward for having suffered my wilderness menus. They ate with reckless abandon. After supper they mosied into a supermarket where Reese Milner and Mike Laine went haywire in the pastry department.

When we discovered there was no bus service between Green River and Daniel, a taxi driver named Curly Pottorff volunteered to drive me back to Daniel that night to get the station wagon. By insisting that I garage the vehicle and trailer at his home, Curly's generous arrangement alleviated a worry of no small proportions at the end of the trip.

Refurbishing the equipment, reading mail from home, and laying in a food supply that had to last for at least two weeks required most of the next morning. By three o'clock we were packed and ready to embark.

"Ship your cargoes, mates. There are ten river miles left in this day," said Mike Kem, edging toward the water.

Throngs of people lined the bridges and roads along the river to see us off. Curly followed a dirt road along the left bank, his taxi loaded far beyond capacity with children. They were still waving when we rounded the sun-blotched façades of the distant cliffs.

Old Mother Green, pouring swiftly down the desolate valley, butting every contour of her trough, bore us along a sinuous, frothy wake and edged us into a region which frightened all of us. Splashing through the regions of her own creation, she seemed to offer a new dimension in solitary majesty. An immeasurably lonely river, she has been despised, dreaded, avoided: a river long hidden from man by a wide thorny swath of no-man's-land bordering both her banks. I felt the tug of her current as she swerved for a last slap at the end of a right bank cliff.

"I think she has a grudge against that cliff," Laine decided, "because it gave us a mile of shade."

At the end of the cliff we rounded a sharp bend and literally collided with the hot late afternoon sunlight. The river took one bold sweep to the west, then relayed the living rumble of stampeding water as her tidal bore drilled

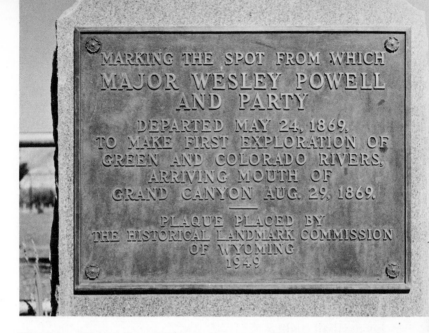

The John Wesley Powell Monument on an island near the city of Green River, Wyoming.

Fossil-bearing cliffs near the city of Green River, Wyoming. At this point the river runs deep and swift. Left Canoe: Mike Laine, fore; Joe Krahulik, aft. Right Canoe: Mike Shannon, fore; Reese Milner, aft.

through a narrow canyon between two raw hills of gray volcanic ash. The roar of rushing torque was no limpid murmur; the air itself vibrated with the machine-like drive of the waves.

We tethered the Leaping Thunderbirds to a jungle of green tumbleweeds and walked down the left bank to read the water. I heard Laine and Little Wolf discussing the excellent campsite above the rapid.

"I wonder why the dickens he doesn't stop here for the night!"

"You know Bob," said Craig with a tone of resignation. "He'd pass up a good campsite to put a rapid behind him and camp on the rocks below it rather than have to dread his devil all night."

The rapid threatened no extraordinary problems for its two-hundred-yard dash, but the shooting pattern did involve a crossover in order to miss a left-bank shallow two thirds of the way down.

"We could run this one blindfolded," Kem declared.

"Don't forget we're carrying twice the weight we ordinarily do because of the extra canned goods. The bows may not lift. If they plow through those crests, we're apt to swamp and lose food." I always fumed a bit that the boys didn't fully comprehend what would happen in the event of a serious food loss; they had never once manifested any outward sign of worry about such calamities. They simply consigned anxiety to my department.

"So," Mike Laine remarked, "we play leapfrog with the granite."

Instead of plowing through the swells and whitecaps, thereby shipping water, each canoe, down to six-inches of freeboard under almost half a ton of cargo, cut an elegant figure as it raised its prow gracefully over the waves. My friend Charbeau had often said: "Only he who has built a canoe with his own hands can fully appreciate this sound companion."

Also to be recognized, the boys' increasing experience in the art of canoe handling was rapidly coming of age; and, much more important, they were learning that this river with her double vintage of joy and disaster—like life itself —embodied far more than peaceful sailing and a passing personal pleasure.

On May 24, 1869, Major John Wesley Powell, schoolteacher, ethnologist, geologist and Civil War hero, embarked at Green River, Wyoming, upon one of the most perilous of all American river adventures. The ten-man expedition, financed by the Chicago Academy of Science and the Smithsonian Institution, used four oaken skiffs for the nine-hundred-mile journey through the Grand Canyon. During their three-month ordeal the party suffered every naked adversity, including desertion, shipwreck, hunger, and death. Yet, his decisions always in the grand tradition of American patriots, the one-armed Powell never allowed any hardship to thwart his purpose and ideals.

Despite certain romantic, sentimental, even poetic, exaggerations in his book, *The Exploration of the Colorado River and Its Canyons*, this man was a daring, bold, brave, efficient scientist. In the unfortunate lapse of twenty-six years between the journey and the written account, many of his penciled notes, taken with an awkward left hand and mildewed from frequent dunkings in the wild water, had become illegible. Events, as well as landscapes, under the magnifying glass of memory have a tendency to mushroom with the years; and although his charming imagination could be attacked on any number of technical issues of the geography and geology of the canyons, the book comprises a unique literary experience.

The names Powell gave to every geographic feature between Green River, Wyoming, and Callville, Nevada, are the names they bear to this day. From Green River to the last day of the trip, we read his words daily with almost biblical reverence.

Beyond the drumming rapid, mile after mile of parched, flood-pared greenscape slipped by, a striking display of inanimate and dazzling vacancy. We could feel the river's hot and humid breath evaporating into the blotter of air above. We watched the moisture condense against cooler masses of upper air and form billowing mile-high cumulus thunderheads to backdrop the haggard hills. Due to absorption and evaporation, the river's volume at this point was only about six per cent of the original precipitation on her storm-born headwaters. It was difficult to picture these sizzling hills in their forty-below-zero winter clothing.

"Hey, look at the bobcat!" Mike Shannon indicated an animal watching us with aloofness from a high bank shelf.

"What's he doing out here?" asked Chip. "This country ought to scare even a bobcat."

"It's his home," Craig said, "and he loves it." How true! Be it a splendid Spanish alcazar of kings or a lonely desert hillside, we all know the mutual animal yearning for that foothold we call home. The beautiful in Nature does not necessarily coincide with man's standards of beauty.

The dry and forlorn hillocks eventually gave way to towering buttes and weather-carved ridges. We camped on the lawn of a wide hardpan ledge with every built-in feature for good camping. One grouchy old bachelor badger begrudgingly conceded us his front yard for the night.

Beyond the mouth of Black Fork Creek, the Green River is the only reliable water available to animals for hundreds of square miles. Other tributaries are undependable either because of high alkalinity, copper salts, or even total disappearance during the long summer and autumn drought. But along the frontiers of this natural bird and mammal wonderland, we witnessed ceaseless night and day performances—everything from monstrous tragedy to the most hilarious comedy.

One of the amusing incidents which I entered into my diary involved a flock of magpies who were power-diving a mother skunk and her procession of six youngsters. We were pulling into a cottonwood savanna for camp near the white alkali mouth of Henry's Fork late one afternoon when we first heard the noisy disturbance. In their initial passes, the diving birds maintained a respectful margin of safety and the skunks behaved as if they were unaware of the existence of the squadron of magpies. If you ever wish to completely infuriate this raucous bully of a bird, ignore him. The longer the skunks disregarded them, the closer the birds dived and the more insulting they became. Instead of peeling off one at a time, they began to dive at the backs of their targets as a unit. When absolutely certain of their range, all seven skunks opened up the most witheringly effective antiaircraft barrage in the animal kingdom. Some of the birds fell to the ground, shaking their heads in silent compound bewilderment. Before they could all recoup their collective wits and dive into the Green for a bath, Mother Skunk rushed in for a final onslaught. The young polecats had magpie for dessert.

On the following morning another event occurred while we were finishing a pancake breakfast. A hungry flock of robber jays moved into camp to case the possibilities. While I was cooking the extra batter into pancakes for the jays, Little Wolf placed a bag of candy in his canoe where he could get at it for a morning snack later on. No sooner had he returned to camp than a jay flew to the canoe and helped himself to a big succulent strawberry gumdrop. As Little Wolf raced back to rescue his precious goodies, the other jays charged the thief and sank their beaks into the adhesive loot. The rolling, spinning, crackling, careening mass of feathers reminded me of a whole package of Chinese firecrackers exploding at the same time. When the birds finally got free, they stood around shrieking invectives at one another and pulling the gooey candy from their beaks with their claws. Leaves, grass, and twigs clung to their feet in an ever-increasing mess, adding to the ridiculous mélée, until the birds finally flew away in a squawking rage. "And so the thief bogs down in his own loot!" was Joe's philosophical observation.

Along the talus slopes of one valley interspersed with buttes was a horizontal bar of lighter colored crust. A short hike disclosed evidence that an ancient lake about the present size of Lake Erie had once occupied this region and the crusty horizontal bands were the former beaches. That the lake bed had been filled as the result of volcanic action was apparent in the flat valley strata of ash that had congealed into great flagstone slabs. When we turned pieces of these slabs on edge and tapped them with a geologist's pick, they broke flat across the horizontal plane, revealing the niche in eternity of fossil fish, shells, and crustaceans. This lake of petrified fish extended from Vermilion Creek in Colorado to Kemmerer, Wyoming, where the world's most extensive quarry of perfect fossil fish is located. The Utes and the Shoshones could tell you more about this lake than geologists could.

Long ago a wicked band of marauders attacked the village of Chief Numah and kidnapped his wife, Natomah. During their flight north, the vandals killed the lovely Natomah. The god Tavwoats was so enraged by the atrocity that he went to the center of the lake and called forth a volcano from whose mouth emerged the Desert Makers. The horde of demons belched forth a pall of flame and hot ashes that covered the land, suffocating and annihilating the band of village raiders, and Tavwoats delivered Natomah's spirit to the happy land beyond the north. But the good Chief Numah remained disconsolate. He refused to believe that his Natomah was really dead and in heaven. To convince him, Tavwoats hacked a deep gorge into the earth from the Wind River Mountains to the Sea of Cortez and built a path for Numah to follow in order that he might have one short glimpse of his bride in Paradise. When Numah returned to his people, Tavwoats closed the trail forever by directing the Green River through the gorge.

Many Indian legends demonstrate that communication exists between man and other animals. Before its long journey north, it was believed that the spirit of the recently deceased dwelled for a time in the body of an animal. Such was the gift Tavwoats bestowed upon Numah's people and their descendants in order that they might get in touch with their departed loved ones. After all, the god couldn't go on forever opening up Green River gorges! But when three of Powell's men, crazed with fright at what they saw and suffered in the canyons, deserted and climbed out to escape, the Indians believed them to be remnants of the marauders who killed Natomah. The unfortunate trio was tomahawked to a pulp and fed to the buzzards.

On July twenty-six we were paddling between the last of the Great Basin buttes, plateaus, and mesas of the Bad Lands when Old Mother Green suddenly fell asleep. We had reached Lake O'Mahoney, the northern extremity of America's newest playground behind Flaming Gorge Dam. The canyon was a spectacularly fissured, deep granite trough that bore no resemblance to a lake.

At first, the experience of moving through the colorful canyon under our own power was fun; but when we emerged into the monotony of low, rolling sage and cactus hills, the feeling of being becalmed came as a shock. As a matter of record, an epidemic of lethargy—a sort of hypnosis akin to inertia—settled over the boys. They paddled as if their bottoms had fallen asleep along with Old Mother Green. As the lake widened, the torpid air of the canyon filled with a lukewarm haze conducive neither to vitality nor to movement.

Scarcely had we beached into the new mud for a rest when an outboard motor began to violate the universal stillness.

"How far is it to the dam?" Reese asked of the two men who approached us.

"Sixty-seven miles and a cyclone of wind all the way," was the answer.

Hugging the windy shore, we paddled between blasts

down the ever-widening body of the lake. I believe the weirdest sight of the trip lay beneath the clear surface of Lake O'Mahoney. To paddle across the face of the mirror and to look straight down upon acres of blossoming cholla and beavertail cactus, sagebrush, and yucca was indeed enough to make one wonder whether or not he might have just paddled into another universe, one where it was normal for trout to swim through a cactus garden twenty feet below the surface of the water! The answer, of course, lay in the fact that the flooding Green River was raising the level of the lake at the rate of six inches per day, and the plant life had not yet begun to decay.

Twelve miles of wind bucking was all our backs and shoulders could take that day, so we beached early on a barren, stony plain and set up an altogether miserable camp. Some of the boys sacked out in the broiling sun for a snooze, others fished, while Mike Laine boiled a nondescript collection of socks in the frying pan.

"I may be filthy, but I'm not unsanitary," he said.

Unable to resist a nearby ridge of screwbean mesquite where I expected to pick up specimens of jasper and obsidian arrowheads, I sauntered across the sage and cactus under the sun's 120° assault. On the far side of the dunes, the playa slowly disappeared into an impenetrable gulf of bristling chollas. A circular and glistening black mass near the edge of the cactus cheval de frise attracted my attention. It proved to be the charred and rusting skeletons of seven wagons, a mute and spectered monument to a tragedy of a century ago, the ghastly details of which we would be forever spared. Yet conjecture would begin every time we examined those arrowheads I found in the vicinity. I was tempted to probe the lost and lonely ruins further, but decided against it; the level of the lake by autumn would write a more fitting final chapter.

After a trout dinner, we sat around the sagebrush camp-fire listening to night sounds—outback sounds conceived in silence—almost loathe to rupture the stillness. The dry, reedy squawk of a great blue heron, the insane laughter of loons, the tinny whine of a cricket fiddling up and down his three-note scale were all shushed and toneless.

In our albums of unforgettables, the nights on the banks of the Green will always be pleasantly recalled, for only at night was the harshness of our experience really smoothed out. The stars appeared especially eager to shine, and the clear, dry, airy starlight itself took on an entirely new meaning for those of us who came from the air-thirsty city. There wasn't enough room in the sky for all the stars, and some of them fell out.

It must have been near midnight when the sounds of the first convulsive vomiting wakened me.

"Who's sick?" I asked as I got into my clothes.

"I am," Chip moaned. "So's Joe."

With the aid of the flashlight, I made the rounds through a veritable nightmare of vomiting boys. I watched the sweat running down their foreheads and through their eyes like tears. For the rest of the night I tinkered with the idea of hailing the first fisherman in order to get word to a ranger for a hasty helicopter rescue.

"Where is Milner?" I asked Kem next morning.

"Down at the lake taking a bath." He must be sick, too, I thought. No one had ever seen him out of the sack before breakfast, not to mention bathing before eating.

The sky was cloudy; not a breath of air stirred.

5

The Flaming Gorge

Our minds and bodies were so distracted by a variety of illnesses, worry, and heat that all our actions now took place in slow motion. No one registered customary enthusiasm either for breakfast or the promise of adventure; we simply knew we had to move on. So we packed—painfully and mechanically—and shoved off.

It is difficult to describe the mirroring, unrippled surface of the lake. If I may use the term, it was dark-bright. Crags of the distance Uintah Mountains to the south raised their snowy brows as if bored by the monotonous stillness, while the welter of rose-colored hilly ridges above both banks of the lake vibrated under rising mirages caused by the heat.

Five minutes after starting, streams of perspiration poured down every expressionless face. A general disinclination toward all effort was plainly evident, and my sputtering conscience kept reminding me that I had pushed them over the rim of their ability and endurance the day before. At the end of five miles of open lake I issued the call to beach.

"I have an idea," I said. Kem shot me a crisp look of helplessness. His brittle disposition generally barometered the attitude of the group.

"Somebody better come up with an idea," he mumbled in an off-key whine. "We're uncomfortable."

"Comfort is for city worshipers," snarled Reese without looking up from his slump over the bow where he was fingering the water. "All people want to do is go around pushing buttons and turning dials." He paused to vomit into the lake. "Nobody ever turns a wheel any more." He rinsed out his mouth. "The power mechanism does it for you—What's your idea?"

"Let's find a shady cove and hole up until day after tomorrow," I offered. The boys all came back to life with clamorous assent.

It was a good idea, but fifteen ghastly miles later, exhausted and mumbling underbreath oaths about slave drivers, Simon Legrees, and the chains of peonage, the little flotilla of discomfort was still without any shade and would be for the observable distance.

At noon we paddled toward a shallow canyon cove along one side of which projected a ridge of cliffs with caves in their foundations. Beaching was accomplished only after constructing a pier with driftwood. As the lake rose, the dry desert clay had absorbed the inexhaustible Green without packing, and for eight feet beyond the edge of the water the new muck was almost as treacherous as quicksand. With no effort, Mike Shannon pushed a canoe paddle straight down to the handle through the warm ooze.

Since it was unanimously agreed that all boys would do nothing but lie in the shade of the caves for the remainder of the afternoon, I went about establishing camp and bringing in squaw wood. Instead of lunch, I made two gallons of Tang and Jell-O drink which Little Wolf hauled away to the boys in the caves. For the protection of food, film, and medicine, I constructed an island of shade with a light nylon tarp. My thermometer, a precision instrument swinging free in the sun from a tripod, uninfluenced by any absorbed heat, for three hours read 135° Fahrenheit! Even the bordering sunflowers and yellow bonnets turned their faces away from that sun.

"You know what made everybody sick, Bob?" Shannon asked as we lay under the shelter.

"No, what?"

"The thought of having to paddle sixty-five miles of lake in this heat."

"We all knew about Lake O'Mahoney before we started. Weather is something no one can predict with accuracy," I reminded him.

At five o'clock the wind sent an enormous gray cloud over to the brow of the cliff. The weather breeder sagged

---

Amphitheater of a former river bend, Lake O'Mahoney near the Flaming Gorge. Left Canoe: Chip Cobley, fore; Joe Krahulik, aft. Center Canoe: Mike Kem, fore; Mike Laine, aft. Right Canoe: Mike Shannon, fore; Reese Milner, aft.

overhead like the skin on an elephant's belly. In the southwest the sun was still busy brassplating the time-fractured
towers of the Uintahs. I felt that lightning was probably
coiled in that cloud, just biding its time before destroying
an aluminum canoe. So I floated all the Leaping Thunderbirds, since there was less danger of a strike on the water.
I'm sure I was not the only one who was wondering if we
were ever to know a concurrence of favorable circumstances.

There was no gentleness in the sound of the rain as it
splashed up little craters in the dusty earth or in the
accompanying electrical bombardment. The atmosphere
smelled of wet sage and juniper. The low clouds drifted
away, their underbellies tinted by the reflections from the
rose-colored hills as the sun finally collapsed behind the
horizon. More hoped for than expected, the boys began
drifting into camp asking for supper and a rendition of
the "Hills of Old Wyomin' " on my Arkansas Steinway.

The stars came out in all their ancient luster while total
silence tiptoed through the hills, a stillness that couldn't be
improved upon. The last quivering sounds of day, more
sensed than heard, vanished as if darkness itself were a
muffler of sound.

On occasion when we felt a need for light campfire
banter, Mike Laine could entertain us for hours with hu-
morous trifles. The campfire also gave us a congenial
chance for throwing into the hopper our plans for the next
day, to revoke decisions when something arose to challenge
their validity, to read Powell's enlightened impressions of
ninety-five years before, or—to paraphrase Confucius—
"where intelligent companions could compose the most
profitable of pleasures." In this land of the Big Empty, the

boys grew quickly to the stature of men or, as someone has said, "declined into adults."

On the morning of the free day, the boys decided to sleep in, get up when they felt like it, and cook their own breakfasts. Although nothing could distract Reese Milner from the serious business of a meal, he had rarely bothered to observe the fine points in the preparation of one. No skimper of details, he decided that morning to "improve" upon the pancake mix with the addition of cheese, raisins, nuts, mashed potatoes, and allspice. The results were far more repulsive than any of the ingredients.

By the time Reese had gotten up, everyone else had eaten and was sitting around hoping for an opportunity to witness the deflation of his vanity.

"How are they, Reese?" someone asked.

"Excellent!" He swallowed the monstrosity with a smile. "The flavor goes with the landscape."

"Come off it, Reese," Little Wolf said. "You don't expect a juniper to grow a pineapple." And when Reese "accidentally" dropped a sizable chunk into the fire, Joe Krahulik laughed so hard he fell to the ground.

As we lay around doing nothing, conversations frequently returned to a longing to get back on the water. With plenty of room in which to roam aimlessly, Kem, Cobley, Laine, and Milner finally wandered off into the hills. The temperature that day remained near 125°, which everyone agreed was cool compared with the day before. Krahulik and Shannon paddled a canoe far out on the flat surface of the lake where the distant orange craft enhanced the perspective. The grit of normalcy had returned to the boys.

Following the day of rest, we resumed with new vigor

the journey toward the Flaming Gorge Dam. Within two miles we read a small one-word sign: UTAH.

Almost immediately the scenery changed from rolling sagebrush to the wide Lucerne Valley, backdropped by the abrupt rise of the Uintah Mountains, the only east-west chain in America. At several points within the valley, Lake O'Mahoney attained a width of two miles. Herds of deer and antelope grazed the shoreline, while elk stayed up among the bright yellow-blossoming sage, blue-green juniper, and clumps of dwarf cedar along the shoulders of the range.

By midday we had crossed the last of the wide lake spreads and were searching among the many deceptive canyon necks for the channel through the Uintahs. The one true passage was hidden at the extreme west end of a large forested mountain that jutted out into the two arms of the lake. Our luck in guessing correctly was linked to Powell's graphic description of the Flaming Gorge where the river had bulldozed one of her several entrances and passages through the range. The narrow canyon corridor with 1200-foot vermilion cliffs made so many twists and turns that we worried for hours that we might be up some box canyon, there being neither current nor any kind of marker to indicate the route.

Walls of five to fifteen layers of up-ended strata of the most brilliantly colored sandstone and shale composed the saw-toothed sides of the canyon through which the Green had carved her course. From the most striking cinnabar reds through shining blues, browns, and maroons, the impression of being overwhelmed by the brutal beauty of so much color must have been experienced by everyone

The Tortuous Channel, Lake O'Mahoney. It was here that Joe Krahulik discovered a way to read ourselves out of a maze of canyons. Left Canoe: Mike Laine, fore; Mike Shannon, aft. Center Canoe: Mike Kem standing; Chip Cobley, aft. Right Canoe: Craig Close, fore; Joe Krahulik, aft.

---

who has passed through here. The tops of the cliffs were crowned with pines, while chaparral grew in dense stands above the ribbon-like terraces of former banks. Far-flung beds of orange wallflowers on sandy shelves competed with equal masses of thistle sage for the attention of swarms of humming birds and pollenizing insects.

The Uintahs, composed chiefly of fiery sandstone, had been subjected to great volcanic pressures far below their bases. The peaks on one side of the river exhibited all their strata with a tilted, upward thrust; geologists call this phenomenon "geanticline." On the opposite bank we observed the downward thrust referred to as "geosyncline." The lifting and dropping began millions of years ago after the Green River had already cut a small canal through the region which was formerly a plain. Her erosive power down through the long vista of time was always at a greater rate than the upthrust, so when you look at the range today and see the river cutting diagonally through, you have to realize that the cutting is and has been taking place faster than the mountains have risen. Otherwise the range would have acted as a dam and the Green would have ended either as a great lake or would have been forced down some new channel around the barrier.

I was startled by a cheer from the boys in the three canoes behind. They had been watching the delicate little canyon swallows, "skeeter eaters," flitting about on shadow-thin wings, prepare a mass attack on a large metal-throated falcon which had designs on some nestlings in their adobe homes on the face of the cliffs.

Big white pelicans with a nine-foot wingspread banked up and down the narrow, twisting gorge. Eagles and os-preys creed at us but didn't bother to fly from their jerry-built nests on shelves and pinnacles overhead. Ducks and geese whizzed by like miniature jet planes, buzzing the Leaping Thunderbirds with wind wakes.

In the Tortuous Channel, a canyon that merited its name, Old Mother Green slept through a deep and dreamy mood, lulling us into an unawareness of any sinister reception. The cavernous depths seemed a hot, humid dungeon in which we were locked up with the great Canyon Maker. No impounding dam would ever bring about her abdication; no combination of barriers—natural or man-made—would ever frustrate the Green.

Fulfilling her ancient destiny through earth's basic media—raw land, torrid sky, and violent water—the Green has left the trademark of her personality upon every exposed surface in the canyon, from the sunshot crags of cloud country to the clawed and riven foundations of the gorge. Intimate little details, still legible on the calendars of bygone centuries, once more assumed importance. But dozens of canyons now began to branch out, and there was no ordinary way of our determining which one would lead to the damsite, there being neither current nor signs. One wrong channel could mean days of aimless wandering and worse. Flanked by perpendicular precipices, the dark beachless voids seemed to yawn for men to devour. Old channels abounded as if the river had rebelled against every course bed her god of gravity had given her.

The emergency alloyed with terror, we fully realized the seriousness of the situation. There were no boatmen to ask, no possible conventional charter of a course through the bewildering maze. We dared not go farther for fear of entering a blind alley that might cost us as much as a week.

"Close with the beach," I proposed when at last a beach appeared at the Y of two canyons.

"How do you know you are in the right channel, Bob? They all look alike to me," Joe said. "But I've been thinking. I may be wrong. Maybe it's worth a try." Joe's surface detachment, cold reasoning, and schooled reserve often distressed me, but I discovered that at least a part of his aloofness was for the purpose of concealing feelings that he thought we had no business to know about.

"It would take a full day to get a bearing from those peaks, if that's what you're thinking," I said.

Joe sat on the aft wedge of his canoe, planted both feet on the seat, wrapped his arms around his legs, and began thinking out loud. "From the third day of this trip we've

considered Old Mother Green as some kind of living being, with a lingo of her own. I think she can talk us out of
this pickle with what she's scratched on the rocks."

Laine turned to Kem and whispered, "The heat's gotten
to Joe. He's blown a gasket!"

Joe ignored this. "See this wall? And the horizontal
scratches near the water level? Almost no weathering. The
scratches in the canyon to the right are weathered with
black stains and sandblasting and lichens. We sounded the
lake a few minutes ago with Shannon's fishing line, and
this channel is over one hundred feet deep. The weathered
channel wouldn't be that deep because it's older and therefore not the most recent bed of the river. So, if we can stay
in the youngest channel, we'll come out at the dam. The
river will show us how to get out by the latest messages she
has scrawled on the rocks."

By comparing the weathered ruts, we found the canyons
where the stream had made her most recent incisions; we
sounded questionable Y's with heavy sinkers attached to
monofilament; and the search became a fun game for more
than twenty miles. Everyone applauded Joe's thinking and
his ability to read the message the Green had written.

We could have bypassed the extra mileage of Horseshoe
Canyon which horseshoed in almost to the center of the
range, but the temptation to glide along the narrow mirror
beneath those 1500-foot walls was greater than the desire
to find an immediate campsite, so no one objected too
vehemently to the extra work. Beyond Horseshoe Canyon
the narrow strip of water resumed a zigzag course due east
for the only variation in the river's north-south course
before joining the Colorado. Although the government
agency called it Flaming Gorge Dam, the concrete had

Reading the river's most recent scratch marks to determine which canyon would lead to the dam at the head of Red Canyon. Left Canoe: Mike Shannon, fore; Joe Krahulik, aft. Center Canoe: Mike Laine, fore; Craig Close, aft. Right Canoe: Chip Cobley, fore; Mike Kem, aft.

been poured at the head of Red Canyon about twenty-five miles east of the Flaming Gorge.

Late that afternoon the wind began drumming a tattoo against the freeboard, so we seized the first lee-side shelf of rock where a camp could be set up. The alpenglow that night radiated wide supernatural bands across the sky: the Utes say that means rain. The discordant wind fingered through everything we owned. Each time we looked up the dark canyon walls into the narrow slit of sky, we saw cosmic tragedies, as meteors fell into the earth's atmosphere. There may have been no connection at all, but whenever we had a windy night, we observed the greatest number of shooting stars and the fewest lightning bugs. Although we never copied anything just because someone else did it that way, we referred to the wind as *La Vieille*—the Old Woman—a reflection of our secret admiration for some of the traits and colorful language of the early voyageurs.

The first glimmer of canyon dawn was beginning to glow when Mike Kem suddenly jumped from his sleeping bag with a shriek that echoed and re-echoed up and down the drowsy cliffscape.

"Bob," he yelled, "there's a vinegarone in my sleeping bag. He crawled over my leg! I've had it!"

Armed with every long heavy object in camp, we crept cautiously to the scene of the outrage. The boys stood poised with flashlights, rocks, and clubs while I slowly unzipped the sleeping bag. With tail and claws held in highest pose of dignity and defiance, an unperturbed scorpion marched out and disappeared under a pile of driftwood. Our collective admiration for his deliberate audacity was such that we refused to kill the dangerous bug.

The wind had awakened I don't know how long before Kem's chilling cry and, by the time we packed the canoes, it was spewing dust banners off the point where we had camped. A motorboat floated ashore to announce that there remained but sixteen miles to the dam. With re-acquired courage we faced La Vieille and the prospect of a short day.

How this region challenged and stirred our interest as the wind-feathered lake widened, thus precluding the necessity of any further rock reading in order to find our way out. There were no ferny dells, no bearded lichens hanging from the walls. Nor will there ever be any receding vales of golden grain along these shores, despite the armchair farmers' irrigation schemes. The Desert Makers had long since abolished all fertility, as witnessed in the dieting cedars and junipers; even the cactus were undernourished. Still, the spacious cleanliness and raw aridity grew on us. We learned not only to accept but to like this kind of uncompromising beauty as we found it. We discovered a measure of exhilaration in the total fatigue at the end of a day's work, and we enjoyed the Green's own brand of blessed, unrestricted loneliness.

About noon that day we met a Mr. Bert Casper and his family whose motor launch was tied up at an improvised landing. Bert, who knew the river, was concerned when he learned that we planned to canoe such notorious canyons as Lodore, Whirlpool, Desolation, and the Labyrinth. We had all read the account of Powell's unfortunate experiences in these canyons, but nobody wanted to discuss them until we got there.

We moored near the damsite in order that I might consult the rangers. We were told that no one in his right mind would attempt to canoe Red Canyon immediately below the dam, that it would take at least two days to portage our gear to the other side of the structure, and that the 3000-second-foot release of water might be cut to zero at any time.

That night we camped on an island where we weathered a genuine cyclone. After the wind, thunder, and lightning, the rain fell in flash flood proportions. As I lay under an inverted canoe swatting mosquitoes and wet scorpions, I got claustrophobia. When the rain stopped, I threw my sleeping bag out in the open where I pondered the onerous portage, the prospects of a water shut-off, and the muddy rapids of Red Canyon.

6

Cataracts, Quicksand, and Dead Ends

"Rise and shine, you water dogs!" I shouted, pounding the bottom of the frying pan at dawn. "It'll take two days to get back into the river. Let's get some gear down there before old King Sol begins to sizzle."

A motorboat beached near the canoes. It was Bert Casper and his son.

"Morning, Bob—boys." Bert wore a very serious expression. "My wife and I couldn't sleep last night for thinking about you fellows. Is there any way we can talk you out of taking these boys down Ladore Canyon?"

"No, Bert. We appreciate your interest, but we'll make it."

"Well, I hate to be a party to what's bound to happen to you, but I'll meet you with the truck over there on the mainland where the dirt road comes down to the lake. I'll haul your outfit over the dam and down to the river."

"But the ranger said nobody could . . ."

"My taxes are paid, Bob. I'll meet you at road's end in thirty minutes."

Twenty minutes later we beached and unloaded at the end of the little dirt road. Then, our loads packed and balanced in the canoes once more, we were about to shove off down Red Canyon when a ranger screeched to a dusty stop at the end of the road fifty feet above the river. I climbed the stony embankment, fully expecting trouble for having allowed Bert Casper to portage the outfit over the dam and down the government service road.

"Mr. Leslie, the superintendent has been trying to get in touch with you. He said tell you we'll release a minimum of twenty-seven hundred cubic feet a second until you get your boys to the Colorado. That's more than normal summer flow. Best of luck!" I could have whooped for joy. I just stood there in the middle of the road, smiling and nodding my head as he drove away.

One minute beyond the concrete tail-water flumes of the 450-foot wall of Flaming Gorge Dam, Old Mother Green resumed her characteristic flow of twenty miles an hour. Five minutes below our launching site, the true atmosphere of Red Canyon, a narrow, twisting gorge half a mile deep, closed in on us.

"From the looks of what's up ahead, I'd say she's in a kinky disposition," Reese announced from the bow.

As we beached and hiked down the rocky left bank, the rapid filled us with wonder. Having brooded and slept in the lake for nearly seventy miles, the river was ready to prove that her integrity had never been compromised. In a long series of violent plunges, she had hurled herself down the deep canyon in a terrifying tantrum of frothy, noisy water. There wasn't an exposed rock the entire length of the cataract, yet the current whipped, lashed, spun, and curled all over the bedrock of her trough.

"For one thing," Joe observed, "the water's deep and crystal clear. If we can get over near the right bank and stay out of those combers, I think we can make it."

Reading a major rapid in Red Canyon below the Flaming Gorge Dam to determine the shooting formula. In the distance are Mike Kem and Mike Shannon. With Canoe: Joe Krahulik, fore; and Reese Milner, in water.

"That's the rough side," I argued.

"But those rolling burbles on this side are caused by submerged boulders. That even choppy surface on the other bank is all side-lash over deep water."

"Okay, boys. By the right flank, follow me!" My guardian devil rocked the bow as I sculled down the slick and splashed into the first white crests. In a rapid, Reese showed less nervousness than a sphinx. I generally chewed a handful of watercress when I could find it.

"Cut to starboard, Bob!" Reese yelled as the bow spray began to douse both of us with forty-two-degree water. The release from the dam was from the bottom of the lake, which accounted for the low temperature.

At the close of each paddle stroke we swung the long-loomed blades in unison as far behind as we could reach, digging deep for sounding, throwing the canoe to the right with every muscle. Reese was on his knees, bending his paddle shank with every stroke until I feared it might snap. When we achieved the choppy sluice near the right bank, all the din of the rapid's hollow cackle was to the left. The shoreline flashed by in a swift, out-of-focus blur. It was a feat of straight-lipped endurance for every foot of the half mile, since the tendency of the backwash was to yank us toward the crests. Then an unforeseen thing happened.

Within two hundred yards of our goal, an up-draft of wind caught the inside of the hull, swung us broadside in a fraction of a second, and slammed the bow into the plumy crest of a three-foot breaker.

"Back water, right side!" I shouted, hoping to swing the bow back downstream. Too late! The canoe shivered from stem to stern under the shocking crunch of the keel colliding with the hidden boulder under the crest. Reese all but somersaulted over the bow. So great was the impact that we lost all our speed, and before we could recover from the shock, we found ourselves flung from the stone and drifting toward the next wave. Another canoe was now bearing down upon us. I had but one recourse. Since almost no forward purchase remained, there was no alternative but to back water until the canoe had turned 270 degrees and again faced downstream—a simple way of stating a perilous undertaking in the middle of a rapid. By some miracle, the bottom rind didn't leak.

Kem and Cobley had watched our close call from a position more to the right. Laine and Close were caught by the same wind but were too far right to be sucked into the crests. Shannon and Krahulik were about half way down the rapid when a gusty blast lashed out like a blacksnake and went to work on them. Joe had studied our predicament and had decided to sacrifice his speed since wind was more apt to veer a fast-moving canoe. Each time they shifted their weight into the swirling wind of anonymous directions, icy water enveloped them.

Each of us was wringing wet and our teeth chattered in the canyon's chilly shade. The sun was now behind a many-storied cloud that had sneaked up to the edge of the gorge for a peep at our activities. Meanwhile the wind left us momentarily to rush up the southwestern wall for a grapple with the pines. We seized the opportunity to push on.

Within minutes another crunching drone thundered up the narrow, rosy-walled canyon. I stood up on the stern seat to determine the proper shore for beaching. On right bends we usually beached on the right bank, known as the slip-off slope, where current was always lightest; in the same manner, on a left bend we beached on the left bank. "Left" and "right," of course, were always determined as we faced downstream.

In the succeeding rapid, the first wave was shaped like a great plumed helmet, and the choppers beyond were evenly spaced for one hundred yards in an eight-foot drop. Two thirds of the volume of the river cartwheeled against a wall of dark red sandstone, while the remainder occupied a secondary channel that would barely float a canoe.

"I don't like what the wind does to the water under a canoe," Chip argued when Reese declared the rapid could be run. With unfailing consistency, Chip championed intelligence against any combination of intuitive senses and emotions, and he considered it no dilution of the male thought to analyze out loud; he never tried to conceal his expressions unless he felt the utterance of them might be harmful or embarrassing to someone. But now the wind stepped in and decided for us. We walked all four canoes down the shallow channel, Reese mouthing his opposition all the way.

For nine miles below the dam, the Green had seen to it that nearly everything in Red Canyon would catch us unprepared. How many of our intelligent performances were due to luck rather than reason, we'll never know. My annuity of healthy fear—and Mike Kem's—paid occasional dividends during certain calculated risks. Some judgments emerged from experience—for this I submit there is no substitute—just as insight often replaced logic when it came to interpreting the chapters of this strange river's story. Yet each problem—blind canyon, quicksand, wind, issues of geology, or a multifarious series of cataracts—had, in addition to a formula for solution, its surprises and its own margins of error.

Having run twelve major rapids and as many minors, and having strung one in the nine miles, we found ourselves mentally and physically exhausted by midafternoon. We were glutted with combat for one day, and every muscle and nerve still cramped at the merest thought of the afternoon's work. As we lay on our sleeping bags, we looked up at the brightly stratified layers of vermilion-hued Uintah walls which ended in pinnacles and spires 2500 feet above.

A water ouzel strutted through a canyon aria on a midstream rock—you'd have thought only an Italian throat capable of such a tune. We had often admired the bird as it strolled about and did pushups on the bottoms of deep pools, flew under water to chase insects and minnows. Little Wolf once scolded a mother ouzel for pushing her

Cordelling the Eleven-Mile Rapid (Ashley Falls). When exposed boulders were scattered throughout the channel as are shown here, we walked the canoes through. Left to right: Mike Shannon, Reese Milner, Joe Krahulik, and Mike Laine.

half-naked children out of a nest and into the chilly current.

Wild pigeons by the hundreds harvested seeds and elderberries above camp, while a pair of bitterns, standing motionless like bowling pins on the right bank, stared at us, first with one eye and then the other. The box elders shook with the hilarity of cedar waxwings that were heckling a big wall-eyed owl who didn't impress me as being very literate. Does and fawns browsed on the strawy skeletons of wild flax and sorrel as they mosied slowly down for their late afternoon drink, but a flock of bighorns preferred to watch from precarious toeholds on cliffs higher up, shaking their heads and stamping their feet at the temerity of the deer. Red Canyon was mossbacked with age, yet so replete with youth.

The boys had begun to realize how wonderfully well the world was put together, how the world today is but a fleeting moment in the grand concept of transition, how results of magnitude are born and grow from the unobservable. That seventy-mile head of water that had been contained behind the Flaming Gorge Dam in but one year helped drive the point home.

By dusk the boys had set up a remarkably efficient kitchen. My chili beans, extended with wild onions, corn meal, hot dogs, and chili peppers—Kem called them Desert Makers' coffin nails—was a veritable canyonland pièce de résistance when topped with mashed potatoes and melted cheese. The peppery entrée set off a simultaneous tirade from foxes, coyotes, bobcats, whippoorwills, and seven boys. A pair of ruffled ravens gargled up the canyon, settled on a boulder near the kitchen, demanded, and received their share.

The next morning we had been under way but a few minutes when the deep bass rumbadoon of savage water reached our ears. We were in fast water to begin with, and beaching along the boulder-strewn shoreline at fifteen miles an hour always offered a major problem in itself. You wouldn't ram a rock parapet with an automobile at fifteen miles an hour, yet this was exactly what we faced. We knew from Powell's descriptions that Ashley Falls must be within half a mile. His account of the river gone mad in this cataract, in addition to the warning I had received earlier, had alerted us as to what we might expect.

A high cliff loomed on the right as the canyon appeared to curve in the direction of the roaring water and a wide-mouth gorge intersected on the left. Before we could do anything about it, we plunged headlong into a short, rough rapid which offered two alternatives: a crossover into a wide whirlpool or a straight shoot down the unknown. Still unaware of the exact whereabouts of Ashley Falls, I signaled for the boys to follow Reese and me into the outer perimeter of the whirlpool.

"Beach as you can!" I shouted as the Leaping Thunderbirds spun around in countercurrent.

When we walked around the bend, the violent cascade was more than obvious. The stream had been compressed against the right bank cliff into a channel less than forty yards wide and with a drop of thirty feet in half a mile; the principal canyon widened at this junction to admit Red Creek. There was no way to read the far end because another acute right angle narrowed into vertical cliffs where the rapid ran wall-to-wall—no beach, no possible chance to read.

Red Creek vomited a coppery foam into the Green at the very lip of the first sluice. This putrid filth the river churned instantly into a café au lait-colored burden which she would not be able to settle out until Lake Powell above Glen Canyon Dam. The crests of the first waves water-wheeled six feet above the trough as the stream poured over the initial fall. Geologically, Ashley Falls was the site of a prehistoric waterfall that the Green had carved down and stretched out into a long, dangerous, and concussive cataract. About half way down the second chute, the river was gnawing the bones of a wrecked boat in which two men had lost their lives a month earlier.

Half-frustrated, half-exasperated, our features and gestures reflecting worry and uncertainty, we read a possible route through which to cordelle each canoe by means of four ropes and the combined efforts of the entire crew.

"Let's get through this first hassle and worry about the other three quarters when we get to it," Cobley suggested.

We walked the first canoe from the whirlpool to the regurgitating mouth of Red Creek. Three boys waded into the muddy, waist-deep stream, snubbed their painters around projecting rocks, and allowed an eddy of current to arc the craft over against the first huge boulder. Chip, Joe, and Reese swam around the rock until they could find footing in the brawling water. Mike Kem and Little Wolf threw them double bowlines, while Laine, Shannon, and I eased the canoe through the rushing water on the outer side of the boulder until we ran out of sternline. Chip's crew assured us they were well anchored. We dropped the lines and held our breath as the current grabbed the loaded boat and attempted to slurp it into the undertow of the midstream waves. But the boys handling the bowlines coaxed and arced the bobbing craft out of apogee and hauled it back to their side of the rock where they held on until my crew could swim around the next obstacle and retrieve our lines. Chip's crew then swam to a new position where this maneuver, known as cordelling, was repeated.

After five similar relays, we reached water shallow enough to wade. But the main force and speed of the river had shifted to this section, so we adopted the technique of heading the canoe between two rocks until it became wedged, the eight of us then lifting it over into water deep enough to float it into the next wedge. The operation took five hours to edge four canoes three hundred yards down the 1800-yard cataract. We were bushed to say the least.

Since Mike Kem and I could endure neither the sight nor the smell of a new gourmet experience which had caught on lately—pancake sandwiches of peanut butter and kippered herring—we threaded our way down to the four-hundred-foot walls at the lower end of the rapid while the others devoured this monstrosity of their own invention. I had determined to swim the rapid, if necessary, to read what we could not see beyond the bend. Before plunging into the full wrath of the river, I saw Mike waving his arms in an effort to get my attention.

"Bob!" he shouted above the roar of the water. "Two things: there's no talus on either side and no noise coming upstream with the wind."

"That means deep water," I called back.

"And if you're gonna swim down there, how the heck are you gonna get back to take your canoe through?"

"That stinking question just decided me to run it!"

At two o'clock Reese and I looked back for one last respectful glance at the wreck on the right bank before shoving off for one of the wildest, most terrifying, runs I ever hope to make. Aside from the grueling pounding, the straight stretch before the wall-to-wall bend was nothing more than dangerously fast; but that very speed, about which we could do nothing but maintain erratic steering, put a dent in the hull the size of a punch bowl when we ricocheted off the cliff at the beginning of the curve. Besides running wall-to-wall, this monstrous gusher included an S-curve as an added problem. The only exposed rock was a giant monolith, an elongated cube twenty feet high, which split the current about half way down the S and took some of the chili sauce out of the river's rigadoon.

There being no whirlpool at the tail end of the rapid, we plowed the bow into the first quicksand cove to get our breath and await the other canoes.

For the remaining ten miles of the canyon we shot the Leaping Thunderbirds across the bawdy laps of fifteen white-water rapids. However, our beautiful river below Red Creek no longer yielded anything white and we had only red-water rapids for the rest of the trip. As we emerged from the canyon, the Uintahs began to withdraw and the river swung into wide valley-meanders with half-submerged islands of silt deposits, gravel bars, and quicksand beaches. The current speed dropped to less than two miles per hour. According to Joe, Old Mother Green needed a rest.

Shannon thought perhaps she was giving us the silent treatment because we made it.

A sweltering heat hovered over the ripening sage whose flowers swayed under the activities of bees and humming-birds. The cool air, draining from the canyon, had soon lost its refreshing sniff of pines but it was still sweet to breathe. The clear afternoon atmosphere, sharpening the distant lightning-whittled crags, brought down the fragrance of the lupine meadows twenty-five miles away.

To the northeast lay the dark, broken mesas and cockscomb buttes of the O-Wi-Yu-Kuts Plateau, a formidably repelling but colorful desert of barren clays, volcanic ash, and basalt crystals. The Green maintained her south-easterly course, snipping at a narrow skirt of the Uintah foothills which Powell called Brown's Park. At one point the river hadn't bothered to go around a spur but had cut the spectacular Swallow Canyon diagonally through the dark red sandstone whose bald cliffs we found stippled with black and yellow lichens and daubed with swallows' adobes.

Beyond Swallow Canyon the river snaked down the valley where the creak of pioneer Mormon wagon wheels and thump of ox hoof still seemed to fill air that hovered above long-abandoned farmsteads. Mountains of tumbleweeds piled at times over the tops of cottonwood groves. The boys yearned for the pines and glittering palisades of the Uintahs, to them a gentler land.

The stupendous diorama of an iron oxide sunset over the Uintah Mountains was not only a fitting glimpse into the gateway of heaven but a fitting close to a stupendous day. No one could gainsay the thrilling adventure of the four Thunderbirds in leaping the white crests, in rounding the corners of magnificent canyon walls, and now in standing counterpoised against tiers of evening color. As I watched the reflections of the campfire on the boys' faces while they re-hashed the strenuous day, I was aware of the magnitude of their pride in the accomplishment. Theirs was a healthy world of work, fun, work, adventure, and work.

As the Green nosed us in on a cargo of sediment from Utah's laundered hills, the state of Colorado threw out a welcome mat of quicksand. The sluggish channel was frequently concealed in a chessboard of silt islands, and we were often checkmated, forced to back up through quicksand and slush.

Rounding a slow bend in the river we came upon one of the most pleasant surprises of the trip: the new and completely modern ranch home of Mr. and Mrs. Dick Randolph. When we had beached the front door opened and out poured twelve small children and two adults.

"Where on earth are you headed?" Mr. Randolph asked after the introductions had been made.

"To the Colorado," one of the boys said. "How far is it to the Canyon of Lodore?"

"About three miles, but surely you're not thinking of entering Lodore in those canoes. Seventeen people have been killed in Lodore lately, worst twenty miles of river on earth." Randolph had been down the Lodore in a kayak, and he knew the channels like the palm of his hand. He took my map, marked the location of every bad rapid and waterfall, and indicated every beach for reading. He gave a shoalwaterman's description of the character of every obstacle while I took careful notes.

"Where do you get your supplies?" I asked, wondering at the size of his family and the excellence of his spread.

"The nearest village is Greystone, Colorado, eighty-seven miles by jeep road. But for anything special we have to go to Craig, one hundred sixty miles each way."

"Well," Mike Kem stated, "except for river rats like us, you certainly must have privacy. Do many people go down the river?"

In answering Mike's question, Randolph looked at me. "The seventeen passed here." My heart skipped about a dozen beats and then tried to make it up.

We shall remember Dick Randolph for what he said about Powell's men: "They gave the most precious gift to their country—a part of themselves—unasked for and not for recognition. That made their gift wholesome and incorruptible."

Then, with the family's good wishes, we moved on down the river to the vertical 3000-foot red walls of the Uintahs, to a narrow slit in the pediment where audacious Old Mother Green had drilled a gate into the very heart of the range: the Gate of Lodore.

7

A Canyonful of Disasters

On the right bank about a mile above the deep Gate of Lodore stood a small sign: DINOSAUR NATIONAL MONU-MENT.

"That's probably the least read sign in America," Reese commented.

We had stopped under a cottonwood for lunch. The afternoon was so sultry hot even the deerflies wouldn't come out to annoy us. A thunderstorm was pounding the inner peaks of the range and we cherished no desire to compete with the notorious rapids under anything but optimum weather conditions.

A number of unfortunate incidents had held us up. In the first place, there were no campsites along the precipitous shoreline. Mike Kem's knee had begun to swell as the result of a wrench he had received while we were in Red Canyon. Then, as if the river was deliberately trying to prevent our penetrating into the canyon beyond the muddy mouth of Vermilion Creek, all four canoes slammed into a silt bar. By the time we got under way, it was dark. For lack of any other choice, we entered the Gate of Lodore in the pitch black of night.

Aided only by the beam of our flashlights, we coasted

along the high-cliffed shore searching for a place to spend the night. The noise of an approaching rapid droned ahead, and I wasn't about to bargain with Fate in the dark, so I ordered a tie-up to some overhanging bushes. We scaled the slippery cliff to a grassy shelf, threw out the sleeping bags, and settled down to an all-night scourge of black wood ants that smelled like Roquefort cheese when squashed.

When it was light enough to see, we relayed the gear back down the cliff and started down the mist-enshrouded canyon. At the first great rapid the feverish river funneled between two cabin-size boulders for a forty-foot drop through one long, roiling, crestless chute. The next two hundred yards of choppy waves were interlaced with rocks and deadfalls, but we had to run it since there was no kind of beach on either bank. The cavernous gloom of the canyon lifted when a steep-angled shaft of sunlight glanced down the valley of Vermilion Creek and searched through the narrow Gate.

The farther down the canyon we paddled, the higher the vertical red walls grew, the more jagged the saw-toothed peaks, the more swiftly the dark current raced. Lodore proclaimed in fiercely carved murals that the unrelenting river was more ancient than the range through which she charged. Every headland that reached the water was the site of an undercut on the upstream side—generally the right bank—where the slough of the centuries had avalanched into the stream, creating minor dams and waterfalls for the river to grind down into rapids with her cargo of liquid sandpaper.

Like all rivers, the Green behaves according to the amount of eroding in which she is engaged, and though

the Uintah Fault is still rising, Old Mother Green main-
tains her trench because gravity forces her to continually
seek a lower level.

Within the second mile of Lodore the deep coulée
broadened temporarily for the admission of a storm-hewn
tributary canyon. A short time ago—say about 100,000
years—the gutted rupture had heaved an encircling block-
ade of boulders into the river which sprawled her out over a
widened course, thus creating a tactical impossibility for
canoeing. Compounding the problem, the cliff-cleavered
landscape hadn't bothered to drop a talus upon which any
kind of beach could form. In contrast with Ashley Falls
where we cordelled between boulders on the left bank, this
unnamed rapid forced us to line through the shallowest
water which ran squarely down the big middle of the
stream. The river was now so silty we couldn't see one inch
below the surface, so we eased along up to our waists, one
man fore and one aft outside each canoe, feeling our way
with the toes of our tennis shoes, slipping from slimy rock to
slimy rock, sometimes dragged into pools over our heads,
but always hanging onto the ropes to prevent the canoes
from slipping broadside into twenty-mile-an-hour current.

By noon, the cataracts, like their devastating waves, had
multiplied with astounding rapidity. There were no relaxing stretches between rapids. A Park Department sign
came into view: UPPER DISASTER FALLS—300 YARDS—
DANGER.

We beached on the left bank and followed the portage
trail through pines and sabina the length of the notorious
man-killer falls whose surface speed attained thirty-two
miles an hour. No longer a waterfall in the sense of a single
spillway, the river dropped through a series of broad ter-

races, strategically deploying boulders against any expedition of canoes.

Of all the romantic mood-tomes ever written about rivers, none has ever come closer to the real spirit of the Green then Robert Southey's "Cataract of Lodore," in which the poet describes the anatomy of an English rapid. It was at Upper Disaster Falls that Powell—incurable romanticist—was reminded of the poem and named the Canyon of Lodore. And because several of Ashley's men were killed here and all his boats destroyed and Powell himself suffered the loss of a boat in the same falls, he named the cataract Disaster Falls.

We had thought Ashley Falls was rough, but we had to re-define the adjective at Disaster Falls. What wading breast deep in swift current, half a step at a time, and restraining over a quarter of a ton of canoe and contents during that first drop of fifteen feet didn't take out of us, the second sluice did during its fifty-foot plunge within the next fifty yards. Half way down the third shelf, we had to unload the canoes and portage forty yards around massive, angular cubes of stone.

When the impasse became insuperable just below the third shelf, we all lost our tempers, climbed into the canoes, paddled up alongside the five-foot combers, and rode out the rapid as if propelled by a catapult. On the way down each canoe picked up an extra cargo of thirty-five gallons of silty water. After a total of five miles in sixteen wet and sweaty hours, no one objected to holing up at a convenient campsite at the foot of the falls.

The only grudge the boys bore against my cooking revolved around quantity. To satisfy virtually barbarian appetites, we were consuming just under forty pounds of food per day. After supper that night, Joe and I made an inventory of the provisions and came up with the fact that we were facing a crisis. Food would have to be rationed until we could reach Jensen village.

The horrendous day closed with the tinny tunes of towhees and the hoarse canyonland ballads of bullfrogs. The cliffs had been fogged in all afternoon, and by nightfall hanging nimbus clouds bottled up and amplified the eerie canyon roar. On my last trip to the beach for a final check of the canoes, I heard the most maniacal burst of laughter from the darkness of the right bank. Shuddering, I played the beam of my flashlight along the shoreless cliffs. The laughter seemed to fade down canyon. When I returned to camp, Chip Cobley asked, "What the deuce were you laughing at?"

I shook my head. "Apparently we're not alone in the canyon. Campers down below I suppose. Sounds are deceiving with that lid of clouds clamped down over the rims. Seems strange Dick Randolph didn't mention anyone ahead of us."

"Could have been a milermore bird," Kem suggested.

After breakfast the following morning, Mike Shannon and I walked down the left shoreline to read the next series of rapids and to see if we could locate the other campers. The river drummed her way down the twisting, fragile gorge in an endless agitation of thunderous arpeggios, but neither campfire smoke nor human voice drifted our way on the morning updraft.

At the foot of Upper Disaster, we read a most disconcerting and demoralizing sign: Escape Route. An arrow indicated—not a trail—but a steep-sided ravine up which

The last bend of smooth water before the Green plunges through the Gate of Lodore, cleft in the Uintah Mountains right background.

Lower Disaster Falls, Lodore Canyon. This is the site of many river tragedies due to uncertain current, submerged boulders, and 30-mile-an-hour water.

only a mountain goat might ascend to the rim. Once up there, a person would be able to go exactly nowhere.

Once more on our way, we shot down the first series of yeasty combers, with almost brazen defiance. A sign soon announced the second twin lieutenant of calamity: LOWER DISASTER FALLS EXTREME DANGER.

The slick leading to the lip of the first drop was shaped like the tapering nose of a baboon. Beyond the funnel of the slick, the river jumped—literally sprang—from her channel, and pitched forward in a somersaulting water-wheel of heady foam. The government portage trail led up the face of the cliff and paralleled the rapid, so we decided to read the cordelling route, if one existed, from above. About half way down the cataract, an outcropping of fingered strata had for several seasons seized on every piece of flotsam; the jam of bleaching bones of cottonwood and pine was stacked twenty feet high; and in a right bank cove at the very foot of the rapid, lay a scrap heap of wrecked boats. During one unguarded moment I envisioned the mound with the addition of four Leaping Thunderbirds, two red and two orange.

Every foot of the 2000-yard cataract prophesied the gloomiest outcome for rigid craft. Both throbbing borders were impassable. We even tried to plumb the bottom of a hypothetical shooting formula by throwing rocks and listening for them to hit the submerged boulders and echo back the depth of the river bed. But the noisy rapid swallowed the echoes.

"We have a choice," I pointed out when we were all back at the slick. "It would take all day to carry everything by trail. That cottonwood log you're sitting on weighs about six hundred pounds—about the same as a canoe.

Let's launch it and see what happens. We may be able to make the other end in a minute and a quarter."

"Bob, you can't be serious?" Reese didn't dare hope for such sport.

"I'll admit it's rash, but this rapid has intimidated me long enough. We'll run this log, then make a decision."

The boys hadn't been so silent since that first frightening glimpse of the Green from the barren hill above the Mormon ferry, where, by any yardstick of comparison with Lodore Canyon, the early miles of the river would be considered a Sunday school picnic on a millstream.

We lifted, levered, and rolled the log into the channel above the slick, walked it to the lip, and sent it forth into the murky torrent. Instead of upending in the waterwheel waves, the missile rode an even keel across each stormy crest. We studied its course all the way to the log jam where it joined its kind. The log, running the worst half of the rapid, did not strike a single rock.

"In other words," Reese surmised, "we cut left between that last boulder and the log jam."

"What do we do about those waterwheels?" Mike Kem asked.

"You can avoid every one of them if you cut left on their sluices," Reese said.

"You can't cut left, Reese," Chip argued. "The suction in their spillways would pull you under the waterwheel and fill your hull in one second. There are two ways to get down this rapid: ride the crests like the log did, or portage the trail. Bob?"

"In my best judgment, that's the way I see it, Chip." During the next few moments I squeezed in a little hard-core thinking. I sat down, slowly filled and lit my pipe.

After careful consideration, I made my decision. "We run it," I said. "And you better sit close to your rigging, life jackets buckled tight. If you get thrown out, swim ashore as soon as possible—any shore. Bowmen will sit aft of the seat. Get all heavy gear amidships and aft of the center thwart. We want the bows to ride out of the water. Reese and I'll make the mistakes."

Reese was visibly shaking and his teeth were chattering as we prowed down the pallid slick, thumped over the baboon's nose, and shot momentarily out into the thin springy air of the canyon. There was less shock and siffle in the abrasive water than I had braced for when the keel contacted the lower rim of the first waterwheel. The shoreline sped by as a dizzy blur. We didn't say a word until we reached the second waterwheel. Just as the canoe slapped down into the trough and sent rooster tails for ten feet on either side, we heard that infernal laughter of the night before.

"What's funny?" Reese yelled.

"Tell you later. Watch for rock burbles."

The suction toward the log jam was almost unbearable. I was hoping the other boys could see the struggle we were having in trying to cut toward the left bank. Missing the ensuing rocks was more a matter of steersmanship than maneuvering, but the rapid was treacherous to the last lisp. In one final eddy of whirling current, the old Lady of the Canyon tried to throw us onto the funeral pile of wrecks, but we read her intentions before the pull became irresistible.

Reese and I dragged the canoe ashore, then ran back up the trail to warn the boys of the suctions and of the supernatural in that cursed laughter.

"What do you figure it is?" Kem asked.

"Probably an auditory illusion. It doesn't matter. Pay no attention," I said. "Remember, it's left in everything on the way down. Fight those suctions to the right. Slackened vigilance for a fraction of a second will dump you into the lap of catastrophe!"

One by one the Leaping Thunderbirds shot, plowed, and plunged through. The efficacy of prayer coupled with Old Mother Green's lessons in self-reliance, vigor, initiative, and stick-to-itiveness had taught us well during the miles before Lodore. We obeyed the river's everlasting code.

"Now, Bob, how about that laughter?" Chip demanded.

"Harp Rapid and Triplet Falls coming up. We'll discuss the supernatural around the campfire."

Unable to read a formula for shooting, we lined down the next three short rapids, running the tailers beyond the initial bad stretches of unavoidable boulders. After lunch we strung the first twenty yards and shot the remainder of Harp Rapid. Beyond Harp we shot four rough ones, reaching the compound threat of Triplet Falls earlier than we expected.

A herd of nine mountain sheep stood on the cliff thirty feet above, turning their heads from side to side as we double-rope cordelled the Scale Six rapid. Except to add an accumulation of pain and fatigue, Triplet Falls was successfully roped within an hour.

The level campsite at the end of Triplet was almost identical with that at the end of Upper Disaster. In regions of greatest silt burden, one of the first jobs after making camp was to fill the buckets with water, since it generally took several hours for the sediment to settle out, although

Triplet Falls, Lodore Canyon. The former location of three waterfalls which the Green has ground down into rapids that pose a triple threat to canoeists.

by now we had quit paying too much attention to sand and silt in the drinking water. When Mike Shannon complained of a polliwog in his drinking cup, Reese told him: "If it floats or wiggles and is too big to chew, spit it out!"

The distant throb of Hell's Half Mile, so named by Powell after his experience with the rapid, and the rasping gush of Triplet filled the night with weird echoes. The sounds seemed to race one another up and down the storm-gutted ravines and became garbled as the wind dragged them across the flying gables of the red sandstone cusps until they no longer resembled the original sounds. From the Gate of Lodore to the end of the canyon, the incessant whirl of movement and the perpetual roar of water permeated every niche and never once allowed us a moment of silent stillness; yet small sounds per se emerged clear and undistorted—the piping of a wood duck, the whistle of a plover, the bugle of a bull elk, even the slurp of a catfish surfacing to gulp swimming frogs.

Reese and I had been the only ones to hear the hollow, haunted laughter in Lower Disaster Falls, but darkness and the wind brought the strange performance to mind again early that evening.

Here, in the Canyon of Lodore we were confronted with several new factors: the deepest, narrowest canyon; lights and shadows that played all sorts of tricks; whirlpool wind currents; and continuous rapids with no smooth water between. Although we had been unable to decode the laughter, we felt certain it had some simple explanation. We weren't about to attribute the phenomenon to the tormented spooks of those who had met their lonely deaths here.

Hell's Half Mile was exactly that. No canoeist on earth could have shot that rapid. Beachless cliffs and acres of monstrous boulders on both sides made cordelling a nightmare. Wasting more than two hours in robust debate, pacing, fuming, and climbing cliffs for ambiguous readings, we finally concluded that a right bank four-rope cordelle was the only choice but for one impossible section. Waist-to-shoulder deep in consistently swift water, we walked the canoes, one at a time, to a shallow inlet next to an ancient, naked, undercut cliff that looked as if it needed a petticoat. For one hundred yards the river ran swifter than ever and ten feet deep next to the sandstone bluff. Beyond the vertical wall, the deep current collided with two dozen boulders and burst into a tawny spray that admitted no passage.

"You have been wanting to climb a mountain, Reese," I said. "Let's go." We scaled the high palisade and slid down the other side, coming to rest on a large flat rock downstream from the cliff.

"Perfect," he puffed. "We get in the canoes, paddle around the cliff, throw you a rope, and you arc us out of the current into this cove. Once we string around those next boulders where all the spray is, we can shoot the rest of the rapid."

"I'll catch the rope from this rock. If I miss, you're goners, so tell everybody to throw slowly and accurately," I said pointedly. "You'll be going more than twenty-five miles an hour by the time you reach here. Back-water as much as possible to break speed."

It seemed hours before Reese and Joe brought the first canoe through. Joe threw the bowline too late and I missed it, but Reese dropped the sternline right into my hands.

Mike Kem, fore; Chip Cobley, aft, shoot the lower half of Hell's Half Mile, Lodore Canyon. It was here that Major Powell lost a boat.

Snubbing quickly around an anchor rock, I pinned the canoe so the current could gee it into the cove.

"We'll go back for Laine's and Little Wolf's boat," Joe said. "They'd never get in close enough with a rope. This is the trickiest operation so far."

During the long wait for the second canoe, I had time to watch a pair of whiskey jacks that were strutting in and out of the heavy spray along the rocky shore. I nearly fell into the river when the two birds hopped onto a nearby rock, faced each other, began doing push-ups, and then gave out with a simultaneous burst of near-human laughter that could be heard for a quarter mile above the roar of the rapid. One bird alone could not have produced that artificial laugh of a clown; but the slightly sour, half-hollow harmony of the two mating calls combined certainly generated a convincing facsimile of an intoxicated human voice. In spite of their being somewhat relieved at the explanation, I could see the boys' disappointment. They had secretly hoped for an array of Beelzebubs and Lucifers at least.

An exceptionally vigorous whirlpool at the foot of Hell's Half Mile finally spun the Leaping Thunderbirds like flotsam onto a wide, sandy beach where we bailed out the gallons of water we had shipped during the jolty, thumpy ride down the last quarter of a mile of the wild rapid. Soaking wet and bitten to the bone by the canyon's misty chill, we stacked a high teepee bonfire and ate lunch before proceeding. I quote from my diary's entry that day:

It was nearly dark and had begun to rain when we finally finished our work in the Canyon of Lodore. Wrecked boats— some ancient, some recent—along the shorelines attest either to the wickedness of the channels or to the folly of those who have attempted them. The water is now very muddy and the silt won't settle out. Its fetid odor is due both to rotting vegetation and to the many animals that have drowned attempting to cross the stream. Tonight, even though we are confined in a deep, narrow gorge, Lodore is behind us; and the sound and fury of rapids cannot be perceived in any distance. All that violence seems so far off as Old Mother Green tiptoes from the chasm with the softest, sobbing whisper, almost as if she mourns the seventeen and God only knows how many more.

8

Whirlpools and Splitting Mountains

During a one-mile sortie out of the Uintahs, the Green flowed due south through dense stands of willow and box elder. We looked back into the tumultuous range for a view of the precipitous face of Zenobia Peak, a 9006-foot crag on the eastern rampart of the Canyon of Lodore. To the west the Wasatch Range of snowy peaks were gathering clouds. I didn't like the several natural weather signs I had noticed the night before: a bilious yellow sunset in frosty calm; a misty rain for the first part of the evening; campfire smoke that dropped and clung to the ground; canyon and cooking odors that remained in the reeds and cattails; short-lived, doleful blasts of pre-dawn wind; silent birds sitting around puffing out their plumage. We didn't need a barometer to read the atmospheric depression. Dark-bellied clouds were beginning to ride in from the south when we reached the Yampa River, a muddy little seepage which added no perceptible volume to the Green when the tributary entered from the east.

Along the left bank of the Yampa was a flat basin which Powell had called Echo Park. Colorful legends circulated among nomadic Indians using this park for winter quarters held that the Green was the former migration trail of the

Anasazi or Ancient Ones between the Yampa and the Yellowstone. No one had ever filled them in on Numah and the Desert Makers.

The right bank, rising opposite the mouth of the Yampa, is a straight, vertical wall of beige-yellow sandstone seven hundred feet high and a mile long without a break. Known nowadays as Steamboat Rock, the narrow formation ends abruptly, like the prow of a great ship, opposite the cottonwood grove of Echo Park. The river makes a sharp U-bend around the prow and flows swiftly north for a mile on the Yampa Plateau side of the great rock wall. A surprising feature of the landmark is that a narrow formation of so great a height could remain standing. The echoes on the plateau side were of such repetitive character that our voices were beaten to death before a message to beach could be relayed from the first canoe to the last.

Before we could break out the ponchos, huge drops of rain began to dapple the muddy surface with little craters of clear water. The cloud that had closed off the sky began waving lightning arms like an excited Frenchman. Following the aerial artillery, the rain whipped the canyon with long twisting switches. One cloud literally tumbled out of the sky and rolled berserk down Whirlpool Canyon, leaving behind the acrid smell of ozone, wet juniper, and cedar duff. Within thirty minutes the clouds had all withdrawn with parting scowls and thunder claps, as if begrudging the sun-flood's two dirty-faced rainbows that hovered over the canyon.

With a flair for the spectacular, the Green suddenly floated us back into the Uintahs and once again into the state of Utah. Both canyon walls were composed of vertical, black, angular columns of hard sandstone whose tower-

Craig Close, fore; Mike Laine, aft, shoot wall-to-wall rapids in Whirlpool Canyon. Freeboard dents and scratches attest to the violence of Lodore Canyon just completed.

ing summits leaned toward the river. The rust of the ages clung to the cliffs and shone with the patina of tarnished silver.

We had sped less than a mile down the dark, lopsided canyon when the boisterous phrases of wild water echoed the familiar message.

"Beach at all cost!" I yelled, the canyon booming my voice back and forth, distorting my words like a powerful public address system.

Although there was no passage along either foot of the austere walls for reading, it was soon evident that the sloshing, brawling water would be deep enough to carry us over whatever had caused the rapid if we could but survive the first writhing waves that were splashing the cliffs on both sides.

"What do you think?" My question was directed to anyone bold enough to venture an answer.

"Right down the big middle," Reese said without a moment's hesitation. "We don't dare get under those cliffs. We'd be torn apart before we could make fifty yards. That leaves the middle."

Mike Laine and Little Wolf asked to lead off for a change. As their bow lifted high over the first crest, I saw Little Wolf reach for water, but he paddled thin air instead. When they slammed down into the first trough, I thought surely he would be washed overboard so great was the volume and velocity of the second wave which struck him across the chest before the bow could rise from the trough. The canoe lost surface speed as the boys stiffened against the shock of each succeeding comber.

Our results on Whirlpool Canyon's first rapid were dismal. Reese and I shipped so much water we almost sank before we could beach. Kem and Cobley duplicated our clumsy efforts. Joe and Mike Shannon boasted only half a canoeful.

Below the rapid, Whirlpool Canyon widened only enough to allow a narrow fringe of rocky beach; the cliffs rose 2700 feet above the river, while the backdrop of Uintah peaks stood 7000 feet above the cliffs. Mountain sheep stared from the shelves of every wall; deer and elk browsed the grassy beds of tributary canyons.

It would be difficult to overstate the experience of Whirlpool Canyon. In one vast amphitheater where the rift of the gorge widened, the river thundered into a black-tarnished left bank wall with such shattering force and volume that the boys declared all the succeeding, down-spinning whirlpools resulted from Old Mother Green's having "bumped her head so hard against that cliff." Even as she hawked a variety of thrilling distractions to tempt the imagination, so she concealed hourly risks. This river had been too long associated with violent forces—The Desert Makers' indigestibles, i.e., volcanoes, earthquakes, floods, fires, drought, and cyclonic winds—to suddenly become a summer playground for little boys.

In sweating out obedience to the fierce simplicity of her code, each of us agonized some during sleeping bag time. Personally, I was never able to completely remove the worry pot from the fire. Exhilarated and fired to accept the challenge each morning, weary and anxious to camp of an evening, by the time we reached Whirlpool we felt inured to almost any task the river might invent.

The suddenness with which calamity could overtake the unwary in Whirlpool Canyon was illustrated just below the big amphitheater. Without the usual grumbled warnings, the current funneled between two massive boulders and poured silently but swiftly over a long spillway into a deep whirling basin that was almost a canyon within a canyon. Around and around we spun, fighting with every muscle to pull the heavy craft toward the outer rim of the whirlpool away from the down-swirling center of the bowl in hopes that the outlet current would yank us from the trap. In one pass around the pool, I decided to shortcut across near the death hole in order to gain speed toward the outlet. Unable to resist a quick glance down the neck of the slurping funnel as the canoe shot past, I saw the bloated body of a deer spinning about six feet below the surface. The animal had been there so long that no hair remained on its hide. The centripetal forces at work in the crater of the whirlpool were so great that all silt and sand had gravitated out, and the hole itself was surrounded by a column of clear water!

Craig Close, fore; Mike Laine, aft, being spun around in one of the giant whirlpools in Whirlpool Canyon. The waves can be seen breaking in 365° of the maelstrom.

Still giddy from the twirling ballet, the river staggered out of the canyon in ever-widening arcs. Muddy little rainbows hovered over the wind-chopped surface as the valley of Island Park spread the two-hundred-yard-wide channel between quicksand islands and windrows of soft silt bars. For nine miles there was practically no current.

We camped on a level right-bank rise called Rainbow Park where we squandered an hour on the unbroken view of the valley from the flame-colored gateway to Split Mountain all the way back to the mouth of Whirlpool Canyon. That night we were favored with an exceptionally long display of fireflies and their glowworm larvae.

Mullein, buckthorn, and goldenrod swayed in a southerly breeze the next morning as we paddled under a 3000-foot overhang to enter Split Mountain. Back into the Uintahs for the sixth and final time, we welcomed once more the timeless spell of the canyonlands. Rose-white walls with interlacing crimson and yellow strata glistened in gay contrast with the somber hues of Lodore and Whirlpool. Pine forests were replaced by sparse scrub cedar and juniper. We ran the first ten rapids without a scratch, but number eleven had to be lined because of a shallow spread of the river bed.

As the canyon continued to widen and the mountain continued to split, the river nosed through a new maze of rocks and weirs. Five miles inside Split Mountain, even the most insignificant rapids were too shallow to run. The redeeming feature, however, was the ease with which canoes could be walked through the lazy flood.

As we approached Moonshine Rapid, the river collected all her wide-flung ripples, directed them into a well-formed slick with a quicksilver sheen, and poured the resulting volume over a single fall. We had barely shot into canoeing formula when another of the Desert Makers' little helpers went to work pushing boulders off the right bank of Split Mountain. Within seconds it looked as if the entire side of the range might crunch into the river ahead of us.

"The mountain's gonna split again, right in front of us!" Reese shouted.

"And dam up the canyon so we can't get out," Mike Kem gloomily predicted.

No sooner had we gotten beyond where boulders were plopping into the river than La Vieille spun the dust of the landslide into our faces, tossed the fixed waves of the rapid out of their rock-marking places, and turned the entire run into a booby trap. We caromed through, but not without scraping bottoms, denting keels, and shipping water.

One vicious Split Mountain cataract goes by the dubious name of Schoolboy Rapid. Bus Hatch, most famous of all western shoalwatermen, once told me the rapid got its name because it was so mild that even a schoolboy could

run it. Bus neglected to say what schoolboy in what craft.
We decided to line half of it.

I don't suppose any stretch of the Green River ever
spawned more hopelessly conflicting sagas of gloom than
the S.O.B. Rapid—the name given on all the maps. There
was, however, one feature of unanimous agreement: it was
impossible. Consequently, every time we heard a ripple
below Englesby Rapid, we jumped out and ran down the
shore to read. In a sudden right-angle bend, the canyon
straightened out for a quarter of a mile of fast, noisy water
that we decided to run since an unobstructed view ahead
presented absolutely no problems. The little rapid spoke in
such persuasive and reassuring terms that, despite steadily
increasing speed and an in-bending cliff ahead, there appeared no symptoms to arouse concern. Still I was con-
scious of an impulse to beach and walk down the shoreline.
"Fun water!" Reese shouted. "If this is the S.O.B.,
we've met a bevy of exaggerators."
At the end of the quarter mile, fifty feet from the cliff
and without a whisper of warning, the perfidious river
plunged over the rim of a dike of sharp strata, boiled up a
hundred-yard convulsion of red death, then half disappeared into a grinning cavern at the foundation of the cliff.
"Go left!" I shouted, back-watering for all I was worth
while Reese dug in off the right bow. That was the way the
river revealed her secrets to fools who disdained to recon-
noiter. Once aware of the treachery, it was too late to get
out. I heard Laine and Little Wolf ricocheting off the
boulders of the dike as they shot helplessly down the
waterfall right behind us.
There was nothing anybody could do but ride out this

most violent cataract of the Green River. When the canoe leaped onto the first six-foot wave, I looked straight skyward at the heaving back of my bowman; on the other side of the crest, I looked straight down at him as we plowed into the trough and shipped twenty gallons of water. The waves were too close together for any rising-falling rhythm. The third or fourth wave would surely sink us before we could be thrown into the cavern's black, slobbering mouth dead ahead. The upper lip of the cave was too low to admit a canoe. We'd be chewed to bits before being swallowed. On the third wave, I almost gave the command to scuttle; on the fourth, I lost my balance and leaned too far to the left, scooping up another thirty gallons. That portside list did the trick. With all the weight suddenly on that side, the next wave threw us out of the stormy crests and into the left bank whirlpool where a high ridge of water sank us within six feet of the shore on the first spin.

Laine and Little Wolf were better off. Mike realized that the waves were too close together to head into, so he swung for a broadside while shoveling away from the suction toward the cave. Kem and Cobley were able to cut left before reaching the first up-ender and therefore suffered nothing more than bruises from the bouncing.

"Ropes ready for rescue!" I ordered as Joe Krahulik and Mike Shannon, looking hopelessly trapped in the big combers, headed straight for the snarling mouth of the cave. In the split second of inertia between crests, Joe accomplished a left turn, broadsided into the next wave, and kept the weight of his torso on his paddle. They sank in three feet of water within ten feet of the beach.

"I was afraid to come into that whirlpool with the canoe nearly full of water," Joe rather half apologized.

9

The Navajo Curse

After resting a day at Dinosaur National Monument and replenishing our supplies at the village of Jensen, we paddled back into a silent river world. Through the valley and hills below Jensen the anonymously colored stream coiled solemnly through poverty-stricken farms and badlands of the Ute Indian Reservation. The Utes are a strong, intelligent, honest, hard-working segment of Utah population, but the land assigned to them toward the end of the nineteenth century was practically worthless. Distances are great, roads and schools are poor; their poverty and neglect have been perpetuated from one generation to the next.

We beached on the right bank in order that the boys might visit a genuine Indian trading post: Ouray—pronounced "You-ray"—Utah, with its single store and the only original log-cabin post office functioning in the United States today. Smiling Ute women sat on benches in the shade of the trading post, while their children played complicated Indian games on the primitive roadbed. Expressionless old men in blue denim shirts and jeans, high-heeled boots, and broad-brim black felt hats sat smoking their pipes on the concrete stoop. Outwardly indifferent toward their perennial misfortune, the Utes are a highly

United States Post Office, Ouray, Utah, on the Ute Indian Reservation. This primitive building is the last original log-cabin post office in use today in the United States.

civilized and cultured people. Nobody heeded the bearded paleface and seven ragged boys approaching from the river.

While we were drinking warm soda pop inside the trading post, a middle-aged Ute struck up a friendly conversation in no gutterally babbled, half-formed syllables. In this man there was grandeur and dignity which shone in contrast with his shabby appearance. He kept hiding the stub of a missing forefinger as if it might betray the secret of some lost battle.

"You're going to portage around Desolation, I hope?"

"No, sir," I assured him. "We shall try to canoe it."

"You can't make it through Desolation Canyon."

"Why not?"

He leaned forward, almost burning a hole through me with his gaze, and whispered, "The Navajo Curse!" Contrary to popular fiction, American Indians were not super-stitious nor known to fear any natural phenomenon, so I smiled, believing him to be pulling my leg.

"Will you step outside for a moment?" he asked.

I followed the tall, lanky native to the concrete stoop where the older Indians sat. "Why can't we take canoes through Desolation?"

"Inuniana—Dineh," said an alert old gentleman. "That means Ancient Ones. They left the Navajo Curse. Four out of ten boatmen have died in Desolation. No canoe has ever gone through."

In ancient warfare between Utes and Navajos, the Ute had some pretty convincing historical documentation as to the effectiveness of the well-known Navajo "dry gulch" or ambush, but we were surprised to discover any twentieth century carryover among enlightened Utes. Yet the thought that the Indians feared the canyon for *any* reason was important to us.

"Would you mind telling us just what the Navajo Curse is?"

We sat down at the invitation of the older Utes whose philosophy was: Listen ten times and then speak only if you have to. They re-stoked their crusty pipes before an ancient shaman spoke.

"The foolish dead have all felt our claims of the Navajo Curse were founded upon the west wind." I sensed in his intonation that he resented disbelief. "The Curse began many centuries ago. Before you enter the canyon, you will see some ancient ruins. What you call Desolation Canyon was a paradise in the days of the Ancient Ones. The river was deep and clean. The hills were gentle and covered with forests full of game and fruit. The Navajos claim their people lived there before the Desert Makers moved in and killed them off. Today the canyon is cursed with rapids; the forests are gone; the hills belch fire; the canyon walls are too high to climb out; no people for over a hundred miles. According to the Navajo sachems, the spirits of the dead Dineh now inhabit violent forces which cannot be overcome. We don't believe all these Navajo claims, but what we have seen in our lifetime would make any intelligent man fear the canyon."

"Where is the old Robbers' Roost country?" Reese asked.

"Nutter's Hole . . . just before the river enters Desolation Canyon about twenty-five miles south of here. Many old time bandits in the seventies and eighties used to hole up there. The Curse got them, too. Brains rotted before their bodies. Gold's buried in caves, but it's all cursed. In one squabble among themselves, fourteen souls leaked out of bullet holes. Never got to spend their loot. Today men lose their lives searching for it."

One by one the old men excused themselves and wandered down the dusty road toward their farms. "This is your last chance to get out," our friend warned. "You're only seventeen miles to Highway Forty."

"Thanks. I have the feeling Desolation Canyon, complete with Navajo Curse, is much less dangerous than the highway."

For ten miles the muddy Green spread out over a channel one hundred and fifty yards wide. Sand bars became numerous, and the fast current often grounded us before we realized we were in shallow water. Gradually Wonsits Valley gave way to desolate hills, sand-drifted dead can-

yons, dry coulées, and a wild panorama of broken head-
lands in a landlocked desert where an unlimited ceiling of
silence seemed to appeal to the interloper to withdraw.

Urged on by imaginations stirred up by the conversation
with the Indians, we faced an occult dimension, this Navajo Curse, which promised to extend beyond the primitive
fact of fast water and hard rocks. Mike Laine was for pooh-
poohing the idea along with milermore birds and vinegarones.

"Your canteen's sprung a leak, brother," I heard him tell
Little Wolf. "In all history there's not one thread of evidence that anything was ever haunted." Mike was such an
objective person that he never allowed himself the pleasure
the rest of us derived from an occasional sortie into the
world of make-believe.

Rounding an amphitheater whose walls rose 1000 feet
above the river, we came upon the surprising little wilderness valley of Nutter's Hole. A flat, closely cropped lawn of
wild rye and blue grama grew beneath scattered groves of
cottonwoods and white-catkined willow as if so designed by
a landscape architect. At the south end of the valley, a
perpendicular red-sandstone cliff rose 2000 feet above the
lawn. Nutter's Hole reminded Little Wolf of a colosseum
with a river running through it. The scene terminated in a
narrow slit we knew to be the gateway to Desolation
Canyon.

During the late afternoon, flocks of doves and pheasants
glided over the cliff, settled momentarily in the treetops,
then dropped to the water where they drank without raising their heads and then flew across the river to forage in
the brushy slopes on the other side. Smaller birds worked
thickets of Fuller's teasel for late afternoon snacks. White

trumpeter swans waddled ashore near camp, their plumage bearing the brown waterline mark of the Green. Deer and antelope, unconcerned by our presence, grazed side by side beneath the cottonwoods.

On a ten-acre plateau just inside the gate of Desolation Canyon, marked by the well-known signature of the Utah sun, lay the deserted foundations of the city of the Ancient Ones. Unlike other Indian civilizations, the Inuniana way of life was not reflected in any vehicle of a story left behind. No canyonland Rosetta Stone has been discovered to key an interpretation of the meanings in their petroglyphs and pictographs carved and painted on the cliffs. That they were of high province Amerind intelligence could be read in the craftsmanship of their architecture, pottery, ornaments, weapons, and mural expression.

From the plateau of the former aboriginal village, I studied the long vista of abysmal aloofness surrounding the cavern-like Desolation Canyon, otherwise known as Powell's Workshop. Experience had taught us that there was always an unjustified fear of the new and unknown as well as the misunderstood, but I dreaded that one hundred and thirty-five miles to Green River, Utah. Aside from the factors of geology, weather, and water, the canyon river would toss our tiny, fragile Leaping Thunderbirds into the tightest, most remote wilderness south of Canada and north of Mexico, where neither help nor escape could be transacted. Despite all the precision and rugged construction that had gone into our boats, they had their limitations as canoes, and by now they were battered and dented from stem to stern. I was replacing sheared rivets and calking keel seams almost daily as the craft bore us over the liquid miles.

Over and above the daily jitters we all felt a personal
fascination in the tonic of the deep canyons where time
simply didn't exist, but where the drive for achievement
and the outwitting of Old Mother Green did. As human
beings we were never exempt from human blunders; and in
the canyon ahead, where one boober meant catastrophe,
lay hundreds of justifications for the healthy dread we
harbored.

We sat admiring the moonscape of curving shoreline at
dusk. The glassy light sparkling on the heaving bosom of
the river held such irresistible fascination that we scarcely
heeded the silently encircling curtain of clouds. I should
have recognized earlier the approach of weather from the
little conversations welling from the willows, from screams
of pintails and teals, from loud warnings of magpies, from
the swans that left the river to hide in the shrubbery.

"Get your gear under the big tarps," I warned as the first
drops of rain began to fall. "Then bring your flashlights
down to the river. There's less chance of the canoes being
struck if we float them. A lightning-struck canoe would put
us out of business."

We were on the way back up the bank to the campsite
when a pronged streak of electricity rose from the cliff to
meet the positive stab from the cloud. Tons of rock showered down the 2000-foot precipice, avalanched along the
moraine, and shuddered to a shaky halt within a few feet of
camp. During the downpour, which was nothing short of a
cloudburst, the wind, whimpering beneath the eave of the
cliff, whipped the rain in every direction.

"The Navajo Curse!" Little Wolf yelled as the boys
crawled under tarps.

"It's so cold I wish I had my long johns with the focal

plane shutter," said Mike Kem who applied a photographic vocabulary to everything.

The storm passed with the same suddenness with which it had appeared. When the rains no longer fell, a porcupine swayed slowly through camp following a mother skunk and two skittishly tripping youngsters. His look of detached boredom and complete disinterest in everything—even the beam of my flashlight—seemed to reflect the grudge he held against Nature for having cheated him out of the enjoyment of close contact with his loved ones.

10

The Awesome Canyon

Sunrise was tinting a few lingering clouds beyond the morning side of the canyon when I borrowed some dry twigs from a trade rat's nest to start the breakfast fire. I left him a graham cracker as an honorable exchange.

Desolation Canyon began as a series of vast amphitheaters terraced to about 2000 feet above the river. Some of the curved formations were two miles in length, varying in color from dark maroon red through blue and yellow to tawny beige. Narrow fringes of cottonwood and willow bordered the out banks, but the water channel passed so near the rocky in banks that neither beach nor riparian growth were ever once afforded on the cliff side.

We had paddled less than a mile when Old Mother Green's gutteral roar announced her first fit of temper. "Beach on the right bank!" I shouted as we approached the lip.

The horned dragon Fear roared from the entrance to Desolation Canyon's first cataract. The slick was too short and swift for any real gain in surface speed. The sluice between the slick and the first wave was a veritable bandit. Instead of throwing us to the left as we had expected from the turbulent brown froth, the undertow deliberately dragged us head-on into the first howling crest where we not only dropped bow but dragged keel on a rock and shipped at least twenty gallons of water astern.

I was so certain that we were going to broadside and capsize in the next wave that I no longer looked ahead; I was picking out a spot on the right bank to which I could swim when it happened. My paddle loom bent each time the blade bit into the effervescent water. Reese fought as I had never seen him struggle before. The little boys wouldn't have the strength to make that crossover unless they could miss the first wave entirely. Avoiding the second trough was a feat to be measured in inches.

A deep-throated bellow ahead—and a clean drop— meant one awful thing: waterfall!

Fortunately the fall was no more than eight feet on a fifty-five-degree tilt instead of a vertical drop, but I felt my intestines turn somersaults when the bow shot out into space as we sped over the spillway. When we hit bottom, all the spray from both sides went away from the canoe and our speed was such that we escaped the rebounding water. I swallowed hard to keep my heart out of my mouth.

We literally leaned on the paddles to brake speed, but we couldn't miss the "depth charge" entirely. The jolt dented the starboard side and swung us broadside. I was all but knocked from the canoe and it took five precious seconds to recover balance and paddling position.

"Hang on!" Reese roared. "Here comes another one. Left! Left!"

Old Mother Green threw another right hook with the mailed fist of her stony gauntlet, but by the grace of Saint Anne we ducked the blow. Fending off the rocks near the lower end of the rapid was comparatively simple after those upper stretch monsters. We beached in soft, warm sand on the right bank and bailed out the excess baggage.

I looked back upstream at the unbelievable drop in the river bed. Chip and Joe were standing on a distant boulder at the head of the rapid, engaged in a dumb show autopsy of our performance. Adhering to our policy of non-interference once the die had been cast, Reese and I unhooked the hondos of the bow- and- sternlines to be used as life ropes if necessary. We scrambled over the shoreline boulders up the right bank as far as we could get, just below the fall, then waded waist deep into the muddy torrent for a rescue should a canoe overturn at the spillway.

Now Cobley prowed into the slick. Instead of paddling ahead of the current, he and Kem elected to back water and maintain what appeared to be a dangerously far right position. Shooting down the initial sluice like a long red arrow, they avoided that first wave which had cost Reese and me our buoyancy, not to mention a badly dented hull. We watched them cross channel to the left bank and wondered what on earth they would do when they discovered the waterfall which was concealed from any possible reading position above. It was impossible for us to get back upstream by either bank to warn them. With ropes loosely coiled and ready, we heard Chip's horrified yell when he suddenly became aware of what the crafty old river had up her sleeve.

At the brim of the fall they shipped their paddles, leaned forward, and gripped the gunnels against the shock of the sudden drop. As a result of that tactic, the Leaping Thunderbird nosed down the flume and lifted her bow cleanly above the waterwheel wave at the foot of the fall. The dull crunch of sharp rock biting into aluminum filtered to us above the deafening crash of the rapid.

"There's something foul about fighting this river," Mike declared when he and Chip joined us. "All her jabs are below the belt!"

Disregarding Chip's formula, the next two boys started down the treacherous channel. For reasons best known to Joe and me—and who isn't entitled to an error once in a while?—Joe declined—or refused—to cut into the left channel beyond the first wave.

"Of all the audacious stunts!" groaned Chip. "He's trying to ride the crests. Get ready with the ropes, boys, to pull out the pieces."

"Hey, wait!" Reese yelled. "Look what he's doing. He's going to miss the waterfall entirely and come in here."

"He can't." Chip was shaking his head. "He's already pounding naked rock."

Bounding from crest to trough, scraping and colliding with every "depth charge" in the upper reaches, Joe finally ended up high, but not dry, on a big smooth boulder. Shipping his paddle, he jumped overboard into the swirling water which, at that point, was ten feet deep, seized the stern, swung the bow toward the right bank, and rocked the canoe off the boulder. Mike Shannon never once quit paddling nor ever glanced astern. He knew his job was to prevent the craft from going broadside. By hanging onto the stern wedge and kicking effectively, Joe nosed the canoe over toward the right bank where the river was shallow enough for him to find footing. Jumping out into three feet of water, Mike joined him and the two boys walked their boat into safe harbor. Shaking his head in a self-accusing manner, Joe stepped ashore.

"Well, I found out one thing," he said as he waded out toward the rest of us; "at last I know what Bob means about fear suddenly paralyzing you. I was afraid to cut over beyond the first wave. I just chickened out."

"At least you didn't have to shoot that infernal water-fall," Chip replied. "Here comes Thunderbird Number Four."

Mike Laine decided to sit on the stern seat, but Craig knelt so low in the bow that all we could see was his broad-brimmed hat, his flying paddle, and swinging spider monkey arms. Following Chip's formula, the two boys succeeded in cutting left and did fairly well along the cliff until their canoe began to slouch into a lazy broadside.

"Right it!" we screamed, realizing we could never make them hear us. I blew the whistle for all I was worth, but they couldn't hear that either. Aware of their plight only when the spillway appeared dead ahead, both boys fought frantically to bring the bow around for a parallel plunge. The canoe, rocking perilously out of rhythm with the river, was not fully on course when it shuddered down the wall of brown water. Leaning all their weight away from the snarl-ing crest below, the two boys shoved fourteen inches of portside freeboard into the turbulence and avoided what otherwise would have been an inevitable roll. Unable to turn the canoe in the powerful current below the fall, they brodied into the first rock which spun the stern down-stream. The shock of the next rock looked for a second as if it might empty the canoe before capsizing it, but quick reasoning, clear commands, and unflinching team work re-balanced the quivering craft. Mike Laine seemed to pivot the entire load as he swung her around, missing all the rocks, and beached. Little geysers of water were

Mike Shannon, fore; Reese Milner, aft, begin one of Desolation Canyon's many turbulent rapids at the spot most remote from roads and town in continental United States.

---

spouting through the hull where rivets had been sheared.

Between gusts we ran the five succeeding cataracts—some a mile long—and strung three during the next seven hours. Without the wind we might have shot them all, but there was an end to human endurance and a point of diminishing returns in mental alertness beyond which even Reese Milner acknowledged the folly of pushing on.

A lateral canyon with 1000 yards of time-leveled moraine opened into a right bank cottonwood savannah that proved irresistible. We had budgeted a week for Desolation and Gray Canyons. One fifth the length lay behind us, so at three o'clock that afternoon no one objected to calling it a day in a beguiling grove high above the terra-cotta flood.

Taking advantage of the remaining daylight hours, I hiked across the alluvial fan at the mouth of the tributary canyon toward what appeared to be an ideal site for an

Indian settlement. On a wide terrace the prehistoric adobes remained only as a semi-circle of bald mounds. The weather-stained cliff behind the ancient remains, however, related an absorbing story. A painted mural showed the Sun God, high above the lower figures, looking down upon the stars, the flat earth, and men with outstretched arms: many ancient peoples considered the stars to be tiny bodies between the earth and the sun. There being neither middens, broken pottery, nor chips from the manufacture of arrowheads, I was tempted to conclude that the site might have been some kind of ceremonial temple instead of the humble homes of a few nomadic outcasts. In the echoes of the boys' songs as they went about their camp chores, I could almost hear the chants of old—incantations to the gods to stay the ghostly fingers of the Desert Makers and the Navajo Curse. I called the time-melted ruin the Citadel of the Gods.

"Hey, Bob! We've found a milermore bird killing a vinegarone and they both got petrified," Mike Kem shouted as I returned to camp. "It's down by the river."

Sure enough, at one time water had filtered between the flat slabs of slatelike rock, had frozen and expanded, thus splitting the stone along a plane that exposed the 100,000,-000-year-old tragedy. The grizzly fossil, embedded in a rock much too large to move, was that of a big scaly bird, about the size of a raven, who had choked in the act of consuming some kind of reptile which looked like a young alligator.

Next morning the boys cocked anxious eyes on the eastern quarter where massive clouds were rapidly overcoming the brassy sun. They were not enthusiastic about leaving a good campsite with excellent shelter to face not only an impending storm but an uncertain series of back-breaking experiences in opposing the fury of the canyon.

We accused the impetuous river of having fallen under the spell of the Navajo Curse, her rapids occurring as short outbursts of rebellious behavior, six or seven to the mile, with deep, slow-swirling eddies in between. Along the shorelines in Desolation Canyon we saw no wreckage of failure such as we had in lesser rapids in the Uintahs. Neither Powell nor that special breed of river men who succeeded him—nor Georgie White, America's first lady of shoalwater—ever had enough energy left after running it to christen any one of Desolation's rapids.

That afternoon, for no special reason, we decided to switch personnel in two of the canoes. The change granted Reese Milner some self-asserting experience and let Joe Krahulik see what a rapid looked like from my bow. During the reading of a number-four magnitude rapid, which the river suspiciously toned down to sound not unlike the rumpling of half a mile of aluminum foil, the deceptive illusion lured us into one of the Green's most savage traps. A broad basin-like whirlpool, without a death hole in the center, spun like a carrousel at the lower end of the fast water.

The heat rising from the sun-tortured walls 2000 feet above had already brought in the choppy gusts to fill the vacuum and to add that extra auto-da-fé to rapid running. My new bowman and I raced down the slick in a moment of steamy calm in hopes of achieving the far end of the cataract before the next onslaught of wind; but a whirling gust hit us about three fourths of the way through and hurled the canoe out of formula.

Unable to read the location of submerged boulders under the wind-stippled surface, we crashed into a slime-covered monolith with such force that the craft was thrown for a sudden high-angle stop on top of the rock. Water was pouring over the stern when Joe bolted over the side and shoved the bow off the rock while I backpaddled and tried to prevent a broadside.

Once off the rock, Joe discovered the water was over six feet deep. Embracing the sharp bow with both arms, chest and belly beneath the canoe, he began struggling over the front end to get back aboard while the boat resumed its pitch down the perilous course. All I could think of during his struggle was the possibility of hitting another rock which would have placed Joe bilaterally on the chopping block beneath the cleaver-like bow. When he was back aboard, I told him about the horrible thought. To this he replied, "I was thinking of a lengthwise guillotine."

Since there was no death hole in the whirlpool at the foot of the rapid, we allowed the canoe to sit and spin while awaiting the other three. Without wind, Milner and Shannon held to the original formula and made it through to the sandy beach without problems. Cobley and Kem were about midway when La Vieille seized the inside of their hull on the down drop between two waves. The jolt flipped Cobley like a tiddlywinks over the stern and into the rapid's churning waves.

"Cobley's out, Bob!" Reese shouted from the beach. "Now Kem's out . . . the canoe's coming through by itself . . . Cobley's back in . . . now Kem's back in! What the devil kind of canoeing is this?" Neither dripping boy had a word to say as they paddled into the whirlpool.

Mike Laine and Craig Close had similar luck. "Laine's

overboard," Reese continued to call the plays. "Without his life jacket as usual. There goes Little Wolf. Get ready to grab their canoe, Bob, I'll swim out for the paddles. Laine's back aboard . . . he's headed for Little Wolf . . . Little Wolf's back aboard . . . they're safe! . . . Grab that paddle."

The incident, filled to the brim with potential tragedy, struck the crew as hilariously funny, and we laughed at the sheer slapstick comedy of the event.

"There's no reason why that should have happened in this rapid," Chip argued.

No one could figure out the ridiculous performance. The only explanation we have ever agreed upon was that voiced by Kem: "It's our first real evidence of the Navajo Curse. Some unseen force yanked us out of the canoes."

"You'd better believe that's exactly what it was," Little Wolf wheezed. "I was grabbed bodily and thrown out!"

We were now in the heart of that region most remote from civilization in continental United States. A sharp-angled ravine immediately behind camp led to the rim of the canyon, so I picked a route up the corrugated wall for a glimpse of the outside world. Overcoming tiers of cliffs by working along terraces, dead moraines, and plunge pools made by the river's former course, I was able at last to view the awful sight which prompted Powell to name Desolation Canyon. I have never known a more sublimely inspiring experience than to stand on that windy pinnacle and gaze into hundreds of miles of primitive stonescape in every direction, with absolutely no suggestion that Twentieth Century man had ever touched it.

Contradicting the impression we got at river level from

looking up angular columns, weathered towers, and jutting cornices, that the stream flowed through a filigreed range, the overview actually confirmed Powell's thesis that the river had cut through the level Tavaputs Plateau of solid sedimentary bedrock between Ouray and Green River, Utah. Here eternity sat and gazed at itself for lack of anything else to do. Thousands of square miles of straw-colored sandstone were broken here and there only by small stands of scrub cedar and juniper, a case-hardened, skeleton forest whose seeds had found precarious footholds in fault cracks between the strata.

On the hazy western hem of the desert rose the soft blue Wasatch Range; and to the east, the dim outlines of the Colorado Rockies danced like mirages above the shimmering atmosphere of intervening vacancy. The mighty Green had her own way in Wyoming, but the very trench she cut became her Bastille in Utah. She was a prisoner in her own corner of space. Perhaps her wrath and fury in cutting the jagged walls was an attempt to escape, but it seemed more in character to think that she had carved the scrolls and oxbows to lengthen her course because she loved her role as heiress apparent to the Desert Makers. Although the thunderous roar of her millstones grinding the timeless chaff was never out of our ears for one moment in Desolation Canyon, from the rim I was unable to detect so much as a whisper despite the heavy, moisture-laden updraft.

From the descriptions he left us, it appears reasonable that Melchior Díaz knew something of Desolation Canyon when he called the river "El Tizón"—"The Firebrand." Certainly James P. Beckwourth (or Beckwith), 1789–1867, an associate of William H. Ashley and one of the greatest Negro pathfinders, was in the area expressly for the purpose of exploring it. His accounts vie with the journals of Lewis and Clark for fascinating reading. Fr. Franco Atanacio Domínguez and Fr. Silvestre Vélez de Escalante of the Bernardo de Miera Expedition, begun July 29, 1776, whose courageous devotion to the Cross took them as far as the musket would back it up, also replenished their water supply in Desolation Canyon. Between Powell's graphic involvement in her history in 1869 and the Navy surplus rubber raft days following World War II, few indeed had been willing to ante up against Old Mother Green's high-stake kitty in the frothing canyon.

I watched the brutal sun sink behind the Wasatch before marshaling my remaining strength to slide back down into the canyon.

We had not known fatigue equal to that which we experienced in Desolation, but the exhaustion was healthy, relaxing; and campfire time was an institution where we could laugh at our mistakes, where we could invent whoppers that everybody—including Laine—tried hard to believe, or where we could just sit around and dream until the chilly wind drove us into our sleeping bags. The contrast between the world of the sun's blazing day and the world of the moon's cold, high-towered night never ceased to intrigue us.

The appearance of a pinkish orange sky the next morning and a steady downdraft predicted the old Navajo sagamore would begin beating his cloud drums and spitting lightning at the cliffs around noon.

"I think this canyon should be renamed the Chasm of the Wind," Joe suggested when La Vieille sprinkled sand on his cereal.

The day was one to remember. During the hours when the sun stood overhead, the heat bore down as if it might be the very breath of the Navajo Curse.

"Have you noticed that the sun has stayed in the same spot for three hours?" Mike Kem included all of us in his observation. "Something's happened. The world's gonna burn up." The other boys agreed with him.

What they hadn't realized, of course, was that we were in one of the canyon's great oxbows where the river flowed from east to west, thus receiving more direct sunlight than the north to south stretches. It was also in this section that we were cursed with tracking eight successive rapids that were too shallow to run. Adding to our misery was the increasingly thick layer of slippery, custard-like silt which clung to every step of footing.

We were riding a deep-water rapid around a 1000-foot scarp when we noticed a change in weather. The sullen wind became less than the breath of a Bessemer converter. When the total mass of cool air had fully descended from the rim, the river's evaporation condensed and we floated along under a layer of rising steam.

"Now we know what happened to Eden when Adam and Eve got the boot," Mike Laine suggested.

Courage and timidity vary among individuals of any group and at different times within the same individual. We were arguing whether or not to run one last long cataract before making camp. The rapid began with an unusually wide slick and wild initial waves impossible to avoid. The narrow trench assured us of deep water, but the speed of the current in such compressed channels and with such sharp drops was always a frightening experience.

The only dissenter was Reese Milner whose past arguments for wanting to run every rapid had at one time or another provoked all of us. "Why don't we run the first waves, then cut out on the right bank to that sandy beach?"

"If we run the first section, what's wrong with running it all?" Chip asked.

"I just don't like the tail end; we'll get sucked into the next rapid below," Reese continued in an effort to bolster his proposition.

"Beyond the first waves, it's clear sailing all the way down," Joe said, indicating an eddy approach to a left bank beach and a choice campsite in a cottonwood vega.

The volume power of the current in such a channel certainly held the grim potential for overshooting the beach. In that case, threading between chaotic waves in the next unread rapid would offer nothing short of bumps and spills. The swirling dark gray sky above the cliffs threatened an immediate deluge and the down-canyon crosscurrents of wind were on the increase. Under any other circumstances I might have strung the entire rapid.

"Bob, we'll leave it up to you," Reese finally agreed, hoping my vacillation would end in surrender.

"We'll run it," I said.

As Joe and I purled across the first boiling eddy and entered the rolling flood of the slick, I watched the wind cuffing the rusty lace on the crests dead ahead. The silty froth clung to our naked torsos each time we received a spumy shower in the troughs between waves. There was one thing in our favor: as the water had thickened with silt, it had become perceptibly more buoyant. As Joe called our course from the bow, his choice reflected his intimate knowledge of the water and how the craft would react.

Despite the fact that three canoes negotiated the rapid

with better than usual results, Reese cut out and beached before the half-way guidon, then tracked into camp. "So I chickened out!" he admitted. "I don't honestly know why. I just chickened out."

We had barely set up shelters when a lusty gale began to spew a fine powdery dust off the desert above. The revolving particles filled the canyon with a horizontal streak of choking sneeze powder which all but blotted out the last light of day.

"We can't say the Utes didn't warn us," Little Wolf stated just before we crawled into the sleeping bags. "We'll choke on this."

The moon became a distorted purple football behind the thick stratum of coppery dust, and its unnatural light wrapped the surface of the Green in red cellophane. Not until an hour before sunrise did our transparent atmosphere return.

Sometime during the next afternoon we slipped out of Desolation Canyon and into the vast blue and violet-red strata of Gray Canyon. The highest vertical walls reached half a mile above the river, and the storied plateau beyond rose another 1000 feet higher than the walls. Although the river generally occupied the full channel of Gray Canyon, there were fewer rapids which had to be walked, so we made better time. The stream sustained little subtraction of water here due to the solid rock bed over which she thrust all her great living energy in one of her swiftest races.

As I watched the well-trained, well-calloused hands in the coordinated action of beaching and unpacking, I realized what this sustained closeness to the river had done

Mike Kem, fore; Chip Cobley, aft, leave the last bad rapid in
Desolation Canyon to enter the first cataract of Gray Canyon.

---

toward perfecting qualities of dexterity and intimate observation that would serve these boys a lifetime. They had
learned to find independent ways over difficult barriers
through the simple expedient of reason. There were times
when Old Mother Green had diluted all our guts, and luck
had played a major part in many uncertain shoalwater
issues; yet the boys were now experienced beyond what was
necessary to know for mere survival.

The crumbling façades of the Roan Cliffs loomed 1000
feet above and two miles behind the rim of the Beckwith
Plateau side of Gray Canyon where the red walls opened to
the west to admit the dark trickle of Price River. The
tributary canyon appeared to be almost as deep as that of
the Green. Intricately carved buttes and long, thin parti-
tions of dark red sandstone 1500 feet high gave the impression of Old World ruins which might topple at any mo-

The boys are suspicious of a stretch of deceptively calm water in Gray Canyon. Left Canoe: Mike Shannon, fore; Joe Krahulik, aft. Center Canoe: Mike Kem, fore; Chip Cobley, aft. Right Canoe: Craig Close, fore; Mike Laine, aft.

ment. It was a region of oxbow turns within larger bends, among cliffs whose many exposed facets from river level to summit showed neither shelves nor breaks. The rimland on both sides of the canyon was composed of hundreds of solid rock mesas whose vertical walls had exfoliated to form angular talus slopes. Stringing or tracking down stretches of impossible rapids was a laborious nuisance in this section, but there were no thwarting impasses during the two days it took to get through.

Beyond the cleavered Gunnison Butte the river went mad to climax over six hundred miles of untamed water. She telescoped every violence we had known up to that time into the last ten miles of Gray Canyon. Quite suddenly the many-storied gash dropped behind and we began paddling the slow, twisting channel of the desolately level Gunnison Valley. A big surprise appeared without warning in the form of a concrete irrigation dam which spanned the river. We paddled to within six feet of the ten-foot spillway before realizing it was there.

"Backwater!" Joe shouted. "The river goes over a dam!" But the current was so gentle in the lake that we paddled across to the left bank without fear of being drawn over the spillway.

"Bob!" Reese called, "Why don't we shoot it?"

"You're out of your mind, but go ahead."

They didn't actually shoot the spillway. They merely slid down the concrete face of the dam, almost capsizing when they hit the pool below. Laine and Close also rode over the rim and half-filled their canoe with water. The rest of us, happily, portaged around. Half an hour later we beached at the public campground in Green River, Utah.

A deputy sheriff was waiting. "Mr. Leslie?"

"Yes, sir."

"I thought for sure it must be a ghost. You actually made it down those canyons in those tin tubs?"

"With difficulties, yes, sir." It was here that we learned to our dismay that Mike Laine was to take the bus home from Green River because of a family emergency.

"There are only one hundred and seventeen miles of the Old Lady left, Mike," I said to the disconsolate boy. "Little Wolf will join me, and we'll take three Leaping Thunderbirds to the confluence. I'll find some boy here in Green River who'll like old Number Four."

II

You Can't Get Out!

Before leaving Green River, Utah, for the final one-hundred-seventeen-mile run to the confluence of the Green and the Colorado rivers, certain urgent preparations were necessary. Most urgent was a means of rescue at the confluence. This had to be firmly established, otherwise we should have to shoot Cataract Canyon's twenty miles of disreputable rapids and hope to emerge in one piece at the settlement of Hite. As it turned out, no one in Green River had the type of equipment necessary to effect the rescue, so I called Tex McClatchy, a school teacher in Moab, who owned a jet-engine craft capable of hauling us and our gear up the eighty-five miles of the Colorado between the confluence and Moab.

"The only day I could make it would be Saturday," Tex said. "That would give you only four days to get down there. I don't think you can make it. The trip's too rough. Of course, you know that once you get in, you can't get out."

"We'll be there, Tex," I agreed. "We don't have any choice. I don't want to run Cataract Canyon under any circumstances. The canoes are getting too beat up."

The people in Green River did everything possible for

us. One man and his wife drove out to a farm and returned with a crate of cantaloupes. Another family volunteered the newest set of maps. Still another offered to house the boys in Moab until I could return to Green River, Wyoming, to get the station wagon. The Highway Patrol, the sheriff's office, and the constable made every facility available to us. A constant flow of visitors moved in and out of camp with offers of help, advice, and warnings about what lay ahead.

One man had an interesting tale to tell, the real dynamite of which lay between the lines of his story: "A couple o' years ago three fellows tried to float down there on a rubber raft. Sank it in Labyrinth Canyon and tried to walk out. Got up on the Forbidden Plateau and were so lost in a day they were never able to find the river again. Tried to kill a rattlesnake for something to eat but one got bitten instead. Guy nearly died. Then they tried to club a bobcat, but the cat just kept jumpin' from one head to the other till they looked as if they'd walked into a bandsaw—a bobcat'll do most anything to keep from gettin' et. Sheriff finally sent a helicopter out and brought 'em back. They couldn't talk when they landed at the airport. Took 'em to Salt Lake where one of 'em died. They were the *lucky* ones. Most of 'em you never hear from again. If a man gets down there without any help, he can't get out."

The deputy sheriff also took a dim view of our going on. "I see your boys are rather badly bruised up, Mr. Leslie."

I nodded. "We took quite a beating in Desolation and Gray Canyons, but at least we put an end to that fiction concerning the Navajo Curse."

"For your information, sir, the Curse extends all the way to the confluence. You'll be in a world sealed off and you can't get out. How do you know Tex McClatchy will meet you when you get there? He has breakdowns like everybody else. What will you do if he doesn't show up?"

"We'll continue down to Hite."

"Over ten-foot waves—wall to wall? I'd like to inspect your equipment if I may."

When the officer left us, I had visions of his returning with a court restraining order that would prevent my taking the boys into Labyrinth Canyon. It was then about three o'clock. "We have less than ten minutes to get loaded and shoved off."

"Is this water potable below town?" I asked a fisherman as we paddled under the railroad bridge.

"Drink it only at the risk of something sprouting in the sediment it'll leave in your belly." He twisted his mouth to say something else. "You guys know you can't get out of Labyrinth Canyon, don't you?"

There being no third seat, Little Wolf sat on a pile of three sleeping bags just behind the center beam thwart so he could shift from port to starboard paddling: "to keep from getting lopsided."

The swift current of the Green bore southeast down the bald-faced valley where the afternoon wind swept the clean, sandy solitudes between scattered clumps of sage. A vapid backdrop of clouds across the northern emptiness of Gunnison Valley screened the Tavaputs and Beckwith plateaus. As the river wound between clusters of blue hills of badly drained clays and hardpan adobes, the sun seemed to expand in the shadeless atmosphere. The canoes plowed three sinuous furrows down the glutted, muddy flood as we paddled ahead of the current. On these open flats we

Former channels of the Green River in Gunnison Valley, Utah. Here the Green has carved her ancient channels through the former landscapes of the dinosaurs.

felt the hot burn of ultra violet on bare bodies, but our sun-tanned hides were no longer susceptible to ill effects. We were all now the color of Indians.

Eight miles below Green River we came upon the magnificent Crystal Geyser whose full eruption coincided with our passing. At its peak, the single spurting spout of hot water and steam was about equal to that of Old Faithful in Yellowstone. The phenomenon occurred on the left bank about sixty feet from water's edge and not more than ten feet above the level of the river.

Despite an ever-thickening burden of brown silt in the river, the sandy shorelines appeared clean and sometimes almost white. We had often held our hands in the water to see how deep within its fertile cargo we could submerge them and still see them; half an inch was now maximum. In addition to her load of silt and flotsam, Old Mother Green packed a load of biological baggage. On her immediately irrigated heaths beyond the fringe of reeds and cattails grew nearly all the annual herbs whose seeds had floated down from the Wind River Mountain meadows. Were a botanical change to occur in Wyoming, it would be reflected all the way to the Gulf of California. That day, the globe thistles ripened and sent forth their tiny embryos by parachute; the whirlwinds lifted the clouds of seeds to the river by the billions. The surface, at one point completely covered from bank to bank, transported the Leaping Thunderbirds along a flowing white flood of thistledown.

Having passed through several minor rapids in a canyon of long castlelike buttes, some of which were actually black, we pulled out of very swift current to camp in a sparse grove of spiny scruboak twenty miles south of Green River. For an overview of the valley behind, I climbed to the summit of a long ridge behind camp. Most of the desert now lay beneath a dark cloud front which was moving slowly south from the Tavaputs Plateau. From my vantage point, the most obvious feature of the distant landscape was the number of times the river had jumped her channel in Gunnison Valley, indicating a variation in her course of as much as sixty miles per million years. Although the valley was less than twenty miles wide, the river achieved much greater length by splaying back and forth across the sandy plain. The mutilated remnants of mountains on both sides bore many levels of her prehistoric scars.

I returned to camp much later than I had planned. The

broad river mirrored the mother-of-pearl sunset over her liquid bronze, while the cliffs to the southeast gleamed sharply against the approaching weather front. We all agreed there could be no substitute for a western sky, but there were practical aspects to consider.

"Better batten down the hatches, Bob," Chip advised. "La Vieille's beginning to croon."

"There are vinegarones all over this place," Little Wolf asserted. "Look what the wind whipped out." He displayed a large, freshly squashed scorpion.

"If one of those bugs nails you with that stinger, you'll feel it for weeks," I warned as we began turning over rocks and driftwood. Everything had a scorpion or a centipede under it. "Put your sleeping bags out on the open dunes or these fellows will crawl in with you."

The boys were unusually quiet, the orange plumes of the driftwood fire reflecting against their faces.

"You know something?" Little Wolf finally began. "I'll bet Mike Laine wishes he were here tonight." Risking the hazard of sounding ridiculous, I suggested that perhaps we missed him more than he missed us.

We sat up later than usual that night, extravagantly throwing log after log on the fire during the meager rain. At length the wind drove the clouds away, and a spastic little moon came out to enshroud the stony quietness of the canyon with a mantle of hollow light in which the coyotes quavered their staccato call, one that always gave emphasis to the silent spaces. The formidable shadow of a cougar slipped down the opposite bank to investigate the croaking of a heron. Little Wolf practiced on the harmonica which he called the canyon Stradivarius. Along with incessant flashes of light, there were loud exclamations and continual moving of sleeping bags that night as scorpions, centipedes, and "flying bedbugs" invaded the privacy of our sleep. I went to bed with my tennis shoes on—fortunately—for the next morning I shook four "vinegarones" out of the lower end of my sleeping bag.

Now the walls of the canyon began to rise around us and the river bore through a deeper and narrower channel. Nowhere else along the Green did we see such dense brakes of drooping willows, thick box elders, entwining brambles, and matted clematis. For miles along the fluvial bows there was not one foot of exposed shoreline where a beaching could be accomplished. Not far down the canyon Old Mother Green was engaged in the familiar, subtle harmonics of a rapid.

"Close with the right bank," I called when I got the first glimpse of the pounding mud.

"What'll we do? We can't beach," Mike Kem shouted.

"Sternmen—not bowmen—sternmen, grab a willow. I'm going ashore." I was about to climb over the gunnel and try to get through the shrubbery on all fours when an entire colony—how many does it take to make a colony?—of rattlesnakes began to hum their unmistakable tune. There was no choice but to submit to the river's savage ways!

Within fifty yards of the slick, Joe and Little Wolf held to overhead willow branches while I stood up on the seat in an attempt to read the noisy stretch ahead. The speeding slick led to a sluice between two projecting boulders which concealed the exact position of the submerged cause of the split current. The heavier volume of rolling water appeared to flow left and then to cross the canyon obliquely through half a dozen stationary crests that barked defiance. Puffy little mounds of red foam rode the merry-go-round two hundred yards downstream.

There was no possibility of cordelling, due to rough and impassable shorelines of ponderous boulders and dense growth. The longer I delayed a decision the more the project took on the look of a failure in the making. Prodded by the urgency of time, our innate fears were magnified to a degree unexceeded in the far worse rapids so many horizons behind. Risking an accident at this stage of the game would be folly compounded. A curious collateral point in this one, not so incidentally, was the fact that the rapid was clearly brand new, the undercut jaw of the cliff having recently disintegrated of its own weight into the stream. The edges of every uneroded rock would be like saw teeth. Shooting this cataract without a comprehensive reading from shoreline was in direct violation of our most rigid rule: *did you see it with both your eyes?*

"The cliff on the right caused the rapid," I reasoned. "Therefore the water's deeper on the left bank. I'm going to shoot over to the extreme left beyond the sluice and not cross over with the choppers. The wind's getting up. We can't vacillate any longer."

The moment we hit that sluice, Old Mother Green came up with her final test. Ruthlessly she lambasted us for the last time with the same heartless fury as the first. Fighting that rapid was about as useless as sending up a distress signal. Having once settled to go left and stay near that bank, we crow-hopped the crests, all of which seemed tenaciously determined to pull us to the right. Had we been unsuspecting, we would have fallen into the trap, with certain destruction of canoes where the main body of current dropped over the slide-created spillway into aisles of closely spaced red boulders. What we did in light of past experience delivered us intact below the whirlpool.

In due rotation came the flat, calm water after the Green River's final rapid—provided you consider the confluence the *end* of the Green River—and the only sound she made from then on was a soft, purring gurgle when she attempted to undercut a cliff.

When our faithful Leaping Thunderbirds had bounced and wallowed through the Green's last rapid and left the noisy canyon behind, we beached on the right bank near the weedy dribble of the San Rafael. This "river" entered the Green as a yard-wide seepage three inches deep. Repeated flash floods, descending from the desert between the Wasatch Range and the Green, had swept away most riparian growth. Wading through reddish slosh up to our knees in order to explore the tributary, we finally reached a low hill for a probe into the desert. Little puffs of exuberant life sprang into evidence all around us. A covey of gossipy quail contested our intrusion and squadrons of magpies and orioles, perched throughout the green belt along the little stream, cocked their heads to one side and rattled off idioms, the text of which even the dullest imagination could comprehend.

That afternoon the river became narrower and deeper, but it lost speed as it took us through a community of sharply symmetrical buttes of loudly differing color and texture patterns. We were paddling four abreast when Mike Kem began to think out loud: "This was an encampment of the Desert Makers. These buttes were their tents —pink, purple, and maroon. It's a landscape where nothing could live but vinegarones and milermore birds."

"Hey, Bob, what's that?" whispered Little Wolf. As he wheeled about on his loose mound of sleeping bags, he almost fell overboard.

"As I live and breathe, it's a milermore bird!" declared Chip Cobley.

"That's the ugliest thing I ever saw," Reese vowed. "It's gotta be a bird, but what kind?"

The strange bird perched like a statue on a rock pedestal and gawked as the crew backwatered the current for a prolonged return stare. Old Sticklefeathers was a muddy white, cranelike creature that stood about three feet tall, had a long curving beak like a flamingo, a bald black head, no tail feathers, and the meanest pair of scowling eyes that ever stared the devil down. It was the rare white wood ibis of the Lower Colorado River Basin.

"Now you wise water dogs who giggled every time we mentioned the milermore bird can eat crow," I said. With which the bird leaned back, opened his beak a yard wide, and issued a ragged, grouchy shriek that filled the canyon. "You hear?" I continued. "That's how he got his name. When he stands on a rock and hollers, you can hear him for a mile-or-more!"

"Hogwash!" Shannon moaned. "Let's get outta here before Bob flushes out a vinegarone!"

Beyond the calico-hued buttes the river slipped noiselessly into the listless shadows of what I consider the most tenably beautiful canyon in North America: Labyrinth Canyon of the Green. For a campsite we chose a sandy left bank shelf in a grove of cottonwoods beneath a Moki cliff dwelling. The red Chinle sandstone walls rose to a height of 1500 feet on the right bank but were somewhat lower and less vertical on our side. The roundly buttressed sprawl

of a side canyon, where the Anasazi had once grown his
corn and squash, widened to one hundred yards below
camp and promised access to the so-called Forbidden
Plateau above. To fire our imaginations, the mud-crusted
wreck of a rubber raft lay draped between two boulders.
The grim reminder of the old timer's account of unendur-
able horror sent me up the box canyon, where I scaled a
sand-blasted moraine for a glimpse into that unfrequented
solitude of bald-headed domes on the dreadful plateau.

Along the rim of the western sky, the San Rafael Swell
lifted a hazy blue curtain beyond the smoldering pastels of
Goblin Valley; along the moonrise edge stretched one of
the most nakedly forbidding, solid rock deserts in America.
You couldn't walk half a mile in any direction without
descending into a 1000-foot dry ravine of thorns, and when
you climbed out—if you still could—you'd be faced with
fifty more just like it. Sixty air miles to the southeast, the
snowy 12,000- and 13,000-foot summits of La Sal Mountains glistened as passing flashes across the hot, quaking
emptiness.

As Old Mother Green snored through the eerie moonscape that night, we sat around the fire and discussed the
dilemma of getting out at the confluence. Even though we
now boasted some elementary literacy in the river's traditions, there still remained many complicated aspects should
Tex McClatchy be unable to reach us. We couldn't sit
around and languish in some crusty brown canyon. I had at
most a three-day supply of emergency food which would be
consumed long before we could negotiate Cataract Canyon.

"Since it'll be a race against time, wind, and food," Kem

offered. "I'm willing to go on short rations starting to-morrow." You'd have to know Mike Kem's devotion to "vittles" to appreciate the magnitude of his proffered sacrifice!

Those who have consciously overcome the obsession of fear, worry, and disbelief have been better men than those in whom the shortcoming was never present in the first place. Yet on the Green River there was neither conquest of nor reprieve from fear and worry for one consecutive twelve-hour period that I can remember. Before falling asleep that night, I lay admiring some winnowing ripples in the moonlit sand drifts; at the same time I was well aware that my familiar old devil Fear crouched behind every dune.

12

The Land of the Sleeping Rainbows

Between the day in 1540 when Díaz, Cárdenas, and Alarcón stared down from the rim of Labyrinth Canyon and the day in 1869 when Major Powell stared up at the same rim from the river, very few white men had looked upon the unique magnificence of the Green River's canyonlands. No river on earth ever flowed a more misbegotten, circuitous course.

In addition to her serpentine route and narrow channel, three consistent aspects marked the Utah phenomenon: first, the Green has carved her swath through an ancient cap of reddish-orange rock which has produced the most spectacular canyon scenery on earth; secondly, the erosive stream has churned up the longest series of violent rapids and cataracts on the North American Continent, thus precluding familiarity; and thirdly, although carrying the most ample perennial source of water in the Southwest, no town of any size has ever developed within fifty miles of her banks.

In the twelfth century A.D. an immigration of timid northern people appeared in the Southwest. They were pursued by a warlike horde that ambushed and destroyed them, their crops, their homes, the very land onto which the timid ones had moved. The pursued were artisans, musicians, aesthetics, and naturalists, an historical fact authenticated by artifacts left behind when final defeat by the warlike ones and by twenty-four consecutive years of drought drove them away forever. Forced into the deep canyon cliffs of the Green and the Colorado, into the concave walls of the mesalands, the timid ones employed the native flagstone and sunbaked mortar to build tiny dwellings high above attack from below and far below attack from above. When the enemy threatened, the cliff dwellers simply withdrew into the austere retreat of their impregnable martellos, reeled in the rope ladders, and remained secure with their stores of food and water until boredom drove the antagonists temporarily away. They were a corn-planting people who longed for permanent farms and peaceful lives, but usually, just before harvest when all the work had been done, the uncompromising enemy would sneak in and rob their narrow canyon fields. From their inner feelings, the dreamers among these Anasazi painted brilliant scenes on their pottery, on the plastered interiors of their miniature dwellings, and, in moods of broader exuberance, on the very faces of the solid canyon walls where, after eight hundred years of weathering, we saw masterpieces created by those brown hands still revealing their messages in full original splendor.

By the middle of the thirteenth century, the pursuers, aided by a cropless drought, won the struggle. The timid ones of the miniature flagstone fortifications disappeared in a dark whirlwind of impenetrable mystery. No one will ever know precisely who they were, whence they came, or where they went. But the story had a logical sequel: with the extinction of the pursued went the disappearance of the pursuer.

One day a boy named Christopher Columbus sat on a *banchina* splashing his feet in the warm April bay of Genoa, wondering what lay beyond the Mediterranean horizon; about the same time a half-naked man of bronze, his woman, and small son, each bearing a deerskin rucksack containing all their gatherings, stood on the east rim of the Labyrinth wondering what lay beyond that thorny gulf. The water they sought was a thin reddish-green ribbon half a mile below . . . half a mile as they might hurl a stone; by foot they were still five hours from a drink. These people were not to be intimidated by any geological issue or by any force of Nature; they were Nature's own children. They were born of cyclone, heat wave, cold wave, dust, flood, fire, drought, earthquake, volcano, war, famine, and pestilence. They feared the genus *Homo*. It was this battle with kind they couldn't survive. The fierce, weird colossus of the Labyrinth of the two rivers—twenty miles across, half a mile deep, and longer than a man could see from north to south—was merely an obstacle-filled ditch with life-giving water at the bottom of the trail.

Silently, unintimidated by the forbidding scene and the steep cliffs, the family descended along ancient game trails into the chaotic abyss. Thirst satisfied, the family rested. It was too late to go on. The man drank again, strung his bow, sheathed a dozen arrows, and crept downstream to stalk a desert bighorn that would also follow a sundown trail to water. His woman and son would have camp ready when he returned with meat.

The flat bench where they had stopped was a quarter of

a mile long and almost as wide, composed of rich, silty soil. The red clay would bake into utensils for cooking and carrying water to the level shelf where the family could plant the corn grains they had carried in the deerskin rucksacks. The cottonwood grove would supply an unlimited harvest of fuel for winter hearth fires and strong vigas to support the sod roof of a hogan. Junipers on the weathered terraces grew aromatic berries; piñons in a lateral canyon showered nuts in early autumn. It was April when the family descended into the Labyrinth. April warmth was bursting with fragrance throughout budland, and in April a man's natural instinct was to plant something.

The essence of the family's vigor was attitude. They had no beasts to bear their burdens, to plow their field, to supply them with food, to haul their harvest, to speed them away from their enemies, no dog to warn them of approaching danger. Their courage, their precautions, their incessant vigilance, their keenly tuned alertness to little sounds and weather changes, their natural harmony with their surroundings were among the factors that combined to multiply their bounty and insure their freedom. Any relinquishment would invite misfortune; they depended upon no one but themselves. They were strong, fast, deadly, and intelligently consistent because of their determination to survive, because they coveted the self-made opportunity to survive.

Evidence that they were a proud people and worthy of their land, their work, their art, their Stone Age life full-pitted against the raw primordium, was set forth in the manner in which they fortified their playa against the erosive river; in the way these farmers of old returned to their soil organic enrichment; in the way these New World

Michelangelos took the charcoal from the fireplace and sketched on the concave canyon wall behind the hogan; in the way they painted the murals.

Life in Labyrinth Canyon, Utah, in the mid 1400s was far from an impregnable retreat of isolation against the vicissitudes which always manifested themselves in those days whenever two families moved within shooting range of each other. Men lived an entire lifetime without ever knowing what it was like to hear the padded moccasin of an approaching friend. A footstep, a shout, a falling stone, a snapping twig could signal either life or destruction or the omnipresent nightmare of invasion. Since no one ever came to smoke the calumet, life depended upon who got in the first accurate shot. The canyon farm, unlike the little castle-builders' homes of two hundred years before, was vulnerable and virtually indefensible. When ruthless, feathered warriors peered over the cliffs and rolled boulders onto cornfield and hogan, there was every prudent reason to re-pack the deerskin rucksack, to jump onto the waiting escape raft of dry cottonwood logs, and to trust Old Mother Green's deep, swift current to bear them away to another fertile bench far beyond, where other ruthless warriors would some day peer over another cliff.

We were keenly aware of an atmosphere surrounding the numerous ruins of cliff dwellings and bench farms of former canyon inhabitants. In the soft gurgling of the river we heard the leathery tomtoms to which moccasined feet had danced so that the corn might mature. We camped near the ruins of the ancient farmer's ruined hogan on his preempted holdings; and we learned to think him a greater hero than the man who drove him away. In these crude representations of his animals, of his sun and moon in the same sky, as well as his abstract drawings, the past seemed to return from the void to interpret for us his smoldering spirit.

Such was his signature frescoed on the canyon wall and soon to be available for all to see. At the time the boys and I were exploring the region, the Congress enacted a bill creating the Canyonlands National Park to preserve this natural wonderland for all Americans.

In addition to the paintings, we often passed petroglyphic messages chiseled into the cliffs, pertified manuscripts of the rhymes of a Pleistocene Tennyson who took that first step between competition of tribe with tribe and the next level of intelligence. Although these artists of the Labyrinth who lived, worked, created, and withered here left no names, they certainly covered the canyon walls with a feast for wonderment.

According to a cobwebby old Navajo legend, the brilliant colors of Bryce Canyon and the Wasatch, Wahweap, and Chinle strata were brought about when the Desert Makers ornamented the western landscapes with stone rainbows. For many generations after the floods had buried the big gila monsters, these rainbows stood as brilliant arcs in the memory of Chief Numah and his beautiful Natomah. We saw many of these gigantic toppled rainbows when the Green took us by what we thought were colorfully stratified, semi-circular amphitheater walls. To the Navajo as to the Ute, this Labyrinth region explored by Major John Wesley Powell and those after him has been for centuries the Land of the Sleeping Rainbows. Thus, when the artist needed pigments—there being no dealer in paint in those days—he dipped his brush in the treasure pot at the foot of these sleeping rainbows.

When Father Garcés, Domínguez, and Escalante faced failure in 1776, they abandoned their small herd of pack donkeys, those hardy, loud-singing, gentle Sicilian creatures familiarly known throughout the Southwest as Rocky Mountain canaries. Now, within minutes of our setting up camp, the solemn descendants of Escalante's little derelicts stood on a ridge high above us and sniffed the late afternoon air.

"I'm going after them," Little Wolf declared.

"Better watch it," Chip warned. "Those hay burners are armed with the greatest accuracy in the animal kickdom!" But in less than fifteen minutes Craig Close and Mike Kem marched back into camp followed by assorted wildjacks, jennets, and colts.

Proof that the animals were still wild came in the cyclone of a disorganized bolt from camp when the twigs of the supper fire were ignited. Back in camp once they were used to the smell of smoke, they ate our three-day emergency rations of cereals which we could not resist giving them, and found can labels as tasty as clover seeds to a sparrow. They never once muscled in on what was not offered to them, but they walked and stood among us as ladies and gentlemen, equally grateful for handouts and affection; nor did they once step on anyone as they prowled among the sleeping bags during the night. I've often wondered at their friendliness, for they had certainly been schooled in the inescapable law of eat-or-be-eaten in a canyon alive with lynx, coyote, and mountain lion.

Before sundown I followed a wide wash up a limestone-engirdled canyon for a look at the blue outer rim of the earth where those fancy petrified rainbows slept. Surely the soul of Phidias was at work on these cloistered walls whose masses and heights could challenge the genius of no lesser mind. The capstone fringe was exempt of sound, while far below all the multiplied voices of late afternoon mingled in an echo of the echoes. Thousands of swallows emerged from their tiny apartment houses to sweep the air clean of insects; a golden eagle, having taloned a cottontail, spiraled out of the canyon, thumbed a ride on a thermal updraft, and soared away to his family. As the final shafts of sunlight slanted through the saw-toothed Wasatch Range, the mountains in the east seemed to rise before the moon.

When I returned to camp, the boys were discussing the possibility of building a ladder in order to get into one of the cliff dwellings and dig around for relics.

"In the first place, there's a law in Utah against molesting antiquity's children," I pointed out. "Why do you suppose they have such a law?"

"They don't want pot-hunters plundering these ruins."

"Exactly. What's here is of historical value and belongs to all the people, not some private collector. When professional archaeologists excavate these ruins, their findings become public property to be preserved in museums where anyone can study them. So it wouldn't be fair play to trespass." The warm light of the fire shone both on the boys' and the donkeys' faces. Their flickering shadows against the rock wall behind produced gigantic, black phantoms. "Barring bad luck, we'll camp tomorrow night on the shore of the so-called Colorado." The statement was a bold one, for the confluence was forty-five miles distant. But it buoyed our hopes.

The next morning the canyon looked as if the giant jaws of a vise half a mile high were about to close on the tiny boatmen below, but it widened within an hour, losing some of the characteristics of a single gash. Dozens of former channels through softer pediment had left a valley ten miles wide, scattered with tall, slender, standing monoliths and monument buttes. Each mile saw new colors and stranger forms emerge, with distant views that beggared human words. Dried morasses had cracked into mosaics of sun-baked mud pans across which we could walk to pick ripe elderberries from an overhanging forest. Even the berries showed the bake mark of the sun, as did everything else in the Southwest.

At the great Bowknot we stopped to look over where the river was struggling to double back upon itself. It had taken three hours to paddle the fifteen miles northeast, south, then northwest, back to the same point of our first view— the longest meander of the Green River's many bowknot bends.

I watched the boys' determined faces a great deal that day as we paddled three abreast. They were never ashamed to rubberneck at the tall cliffs like country boys on a first trip to a city, nor were they immune to small thrills: a pair of harmonizing finches or a black-headed merganser beaking her young, one at a time, from a nest in a cottonwood, urging them onto the water. Topics for discussion revolved with sensitive intelligence around our relationship with Old Mother Green's country. Our mentor's most precious gift to the boys was a good beginning in knowing themselves.

Toward the geological end of what Powell called the Labyrinth, we came upon 1500-foot cliffs of dark red Wahweap formation high above the right bank near a bend in

The Navajos and Utes called these colorfully stratified amphitheater bends "sleeping rainbows." Southwestern Utah has been known for generations as the Land of the Sleeping Rainbows; the same region is now known as Canyonlands National Park.

---

the canyon. Here the wind was chiseling an embryonic arch shaped like the outer human ear.

"Does it have a name?" Little Wolf asked.

"Not according to the maps."

"Then let's call it the Ear-of-the-Wind, because that's what it was to the Anasazi on the left bank. Listen!" Craig's words came drifting back to us without the slightest distortion.

A deep-slashed, dry-wash ravine opened out onto a wide fan moraine on the left bank where there had been a farm centuries before. Like his relative upstream, the canyon

Craig Close called this embryonic arch in Labyrinth Canyon the "Ear of the Wind" because it picked up our words and whispered them back to us.

dweller was without dogs to warn him of approaching danger; but the sleepless escarpments always collected every sound that descended the chasm, and so warned with unfailing accuracy when arrows were about to fly. Subsequent nomads wandered in and remained for a time, then migrated into extinction, leaving behind—like the cliff dwellers before the farmers—mysterious fantasies that have fascinated Twentieth Century storytellers.

Since that incalculable distance when man first stood on two feet with hands free to do things not associated with feet, he has left the initials of his spiritual and intellectual needs on cliffs, in caves, on his utensils; and the wealth of these remains in Labyrinth and Stillwater Canyons caught and held our fancy with almost unbroken attention as the Leaping Thunderbirds bounced, plowed, and wallowed through to the confluence.

Another taste acquired as we glided down these last miles of the journey reflected a more sophisticated and rigorous analysis of Old Mother Green's wonderfully systematic behavior as she went about fulfilling her mission. Not only was this her world of natural wonders, abundantly and effortlessly wrought after the Desert Makers had used all their land, but it was also a realm of climaxes to test our ingenuity and mettle in areas of meanings deeper than those fathered during the days when basic survival consumed so much of our energy that we had little inclination to explore more subtle regions. We were not seeking any grotesque occult or supernatural answers. We were simply in love with this corner of the west, and, accordingly, with the way those wide horizons broadened our own appreciation and comprehension of what lay within the subdivisions of the Green's natural destiny. We began to assess our own lives in terms of the life of a river.

I often contrasted our work on the Green with the slow-paced canoeing on Canadian lakes or on sluggishly mature old streams like the River Clyde where I once paddled near a relative's ancestral home in Scotland. The Green along every mile of her length was different. Her hazards were greater, her price higher, her allies of weather and desert more violent, her scenery more spectacular, her harvest of satisfaction and her feast far more abundant than that of any river I have ever worked.

The fact that the Green from her most ancient beginnings was and still is a single river and not a system of rivers—from source to confluence with the Colorado—is the conclusive characteristic which has marked her as unique on this continent. Powell himself admitted that the

line separating Labyrinth Canyon and Stillwater Canyon
was but an imaginary one since there was no real separation
into two canyons. As Stillwater became deeper, the river
occupied more and more of the channel, until the water
ran wall-to-wall with few places to beach. The vertical
heights swung and twisted through 360 degrees of the
compass. Beyond the rim of the right bank for as far as we
could see in any direction lay the Land of Standing Rocks,
a region of gaily colored buttes, mesas, cliffs, pinnacles,
shafts, terraces, and domes of rock without vegetation. In
each amphitheater bend a stone rainbow stretched, 1500
feet high and half a mile long. We came upon several
former bowknot bends where the river had worn away the
soft rock at the narrows and had taken the short cut,
leaving mammoth circular abutment towers high and dry.

The depth, color, and variety of landscape forms in the
confluence area as viewed from Dead Horse Point and
Grand View Point—heart of Canyonlands National Park
—have been compared with the Grand Canyon of the
Colorado. Technically, from the standpoint of size, the
Grand Canyon could be swallowed up and lost in the Canyonlands. As for color, river views, and geomorphic forms,
no landscape can justly be compared with the confluence
country. In my humble opinion, the most spectacular phenomenon in America lies between Dead Horse Point and
the sublimely inspiring horizon to the southwest. Here a
single view encompasses 10,000 square miles of snow-
topped peaks over 13,000 feet above sea level; of pine,
juniper, and aspen forests; of limitlessly hued desert; of one
hundred radiantly shining canyons; of the two mighty
rivers that created the scene; and of the far-flung petrified
rainbows which sleep in the wake of time.

General panorama of the Colorado River from Dead Horse Point, Canyonlands National Park. Green River located near left skyline.

Leaning forward with eager curiosity, the boys paddled toward a six-foot human skull carved with remarkable fidelity in rock which lay half-submerged on the left bank. The water snickered in the hollow eye sockets as we closed with the shore for a photograph. We wondered whether this macabre memento was Old Mother Green's own monument to those upon whom she had laid her lethal claims, or whether she referred to the consequences of the uranium mine on the Blue Hill shelf nearby where they extracted the ore in 1905 and sent it off to Madame Curie. It was Joe Krahulik who commented: "Beware of disturbing the materials in the tombs of the Desert Makers!"

During the final twenty miles, the canyon walls reached

Skull Rock, Stillwater Canyon, near the site of the first uranium mine (Blue Shelf). Joe Krahulik interpreted the sinister implications as a warning to those who disturb the tombs of the Desert Makers.

higher and higher overhead, with fewer breaks and no possibility of scaling for a view of the rim world. The white Colorado capstone glistened almost like snow on both sunny ridges. One hundred miles south of Green River the current seized the Leaping Thunderbirds and plummeted them forward with a hurtling thrust we had not known since Gray Canyon. Then, as the perilously curving red abyss deepened and the channel narrowed, the water of confused color slid on, flat and glossy with a sparkle of revolving mica, and there was not a ripple, not a sound, as the mighty stream flowed wall-to-wall. Steering was so sensitive to pressure that a delicate flick of the wrist would send a canoe effortlessly from one bank to the other. Although the sun penetrated the 2000-foot gash only on east-west bends, the shadows were lighted by reflection and therefore possessed with character and personality. The foot candle power light readings on the Weston meter scale remained constant at eight hundred under a narrow strip of sapphire sky—the bluest living blue I ever hope to see.

Rounding the last bend, Old Mother Green shot down a quarter-mile straight homestretch which appeared to end against the blank wall of a vertical 1300-foot cliff. At the Y of the Green and the Colorado, the former stream, flowing with more than twice the volume of the Colorado, seemed to ignore and push aside her greatest tributary as she rushed in for a grinding bite at the left bank cliff. Carrying a ton of dissolved salts per acre-foot and a million tons of silt per day, the Green was reluctant to meld with the Colorado's less turbid water; and a long, distinguishing line three quarters of the way across extended down into Cataract Canyon where twenty miles of churning rapids would homogenize the two waters before their settling rest in Lake Powell behind Glen Canyon Dam.

"We made it!" Little Wolf shouted as we beached on the broad, dry silt bar of the right bank, one hundred yards below the confluence, one of the finest campsites of the entire trip.

"First canoes to do the total length of the Green River!" whooped Reese as he skittered about the clean yellow sand and threw his hat into the air.

"We aren't out of here yet," Joe warned. There was an ominous tone in his voice which sobered our jubilation. "Twenty miles of the worst rapids are ahead if Tex doesn't show. We're eighty miles from the nearest civilization."

13

Historical Mistake

The spacious floor of the hard silt terrace on the right bank butted up to a dense grove of box elders and willows above which lay a sagebrush bench, narrower and shorter than the one on which we camped. The limestone cliff above the last terrace had crumbled into a choppy moraine which, from camp, seemed to disappear into the sky itself. A preliminary examination lent some hope that the rim of the canyon might be achieved up the shattered crevices of the moraine.

In 1869 Major Powell had camped on the exact same spot for three days before continuing his fruitful journey into Grand Canyon. From this site we hoped to verify or nullify the theory that the Colorado was in fact a tributary of the Green. Several superficial factors pointed favorably toward the theory. Despite two dams, the Flaming Gorge and the Fontenelle, the Green poured twice the volume of water into the confluence as did the Colorado with no dams. In addition to the U.S. Department of the Interior projects on the main stem of the Green, there were seven reclamation dams on tributaries in the upper reaches which deprived the river of subaltern feeders. Average flow of the Green River between 1914 and 1964 for the months of

July and August varied from four hundred second-feet in drought years to 11,700 second-feet in wet years with a theoretical average of about 5000 second-feet. The Colorado, during the same period, averaged two hundred second-feet in drought years to 10,500 second-feet in wet years with a theoretical average of about 2000 second-feet: a disparity indicating the Colorado to be only two fifths the stream the Green was over the fifty years during which the measurements were taken. We had paddled into Green River, Wyoming, on a flood flow of 10,500 second-feet on July 24, 1964, and into the confluence a month later on 2500 controlled second-feet. With the Colorado's approximate 1200 second-feet, the two streams poured less than 4000 second-feet into Lake Powell during August, the driest month. The Green's excess flood, of course, lay impounded in Lake O'Mahoney.

The second factor favoring the theory that the Green was indeed the main stream was manifest for even the most uninitiated to see in the actual history of the two river beds at the confluence. Fortunately for the sake of our argument, the strata near water level lay horizontally parallel with the two rivers. Suffice it to say, the incision made by the Green was visibly deeper than that made by the Colorado, which indicated that the Green was the older river. In all fairness to the unresolved issue, however, I should point out that both streams have cut their canyons about equally. Up to now, geologists have not been able to agree on the comparative geologic ages of Green River Lake, source of the Green, and Grand Lake, source of the Colorado, although they do agree that the two sources are approximately the same age. Major Powell sidestepped the issue neatly during his tenure as Chief of the Geological Survey simply by referring to the Grand River—that part of the Colorado above the confluence was called the Grand up until a few years ago—and the Green River as flowing together to form the Colorado.

For a comprehensive photograph of the confluence, one that would show the exposed strata, the comparative sizes of the two streams, and the general lay of the land, it was apparent that we should be obliged at all costs to scale the moraine on the southwest bank of the Y and there use the Leica's wide-angle lens.

As a special goodie that night, I rolled out pie-crust dough into the shape of large tortillas, sprinkled allspice on the inner surface, spread a filling of peach jam, folded and kneaded the edges together to form a half moon, and fried the tarts until brown. The result: fried pies which the boys called "Green River Belly Busters."

Yet, regardless of activity in which we engaged, there was one sinister thought uppermost in our minds: "Would Tex McClatchy make it?" Even with all those miles of whitewater experience under our belts, no one wanted to face Cataract Canyon. The moon wore a smile that night as it rose and smeared the Canyon of the Colorado with cold light.

"All uncertainties but one are behind us," Chip remarked as we sat on driftwood logs around what we hoped would be the last campfire. I sensed several interior tremors of doubt. The canyon seemed so deep and dark and far away; some would term it loneliness and emptiness on a scale too vast to tolerate.

"Still you hate to leave it," Joe said, "to return to the salt mines of freedom. It'll be hard to obey your conscience during the winter months of the work-a-day world when the freeway swish will fill your ears with a sound something like the music of the wild water."

"And when you look out over the city," Reese added, "just remember these nights when we couldn't see an electric light in any distance." What the wrinkled old canyons lacked in bodily comforts, they made up in provisions for the soul. They had altered immeasurably certain attitudes of eight modern canoeists. What spells they must have cast on primitive minds inhabiting the cliffs, shelves, and islands!

"I like the bonuses of this trip," Little Wolf mused. "It's been a sweatshop all the way, but there's always been a bonus—schools for decoys, songs of the ouzels, the Anasazi artists, the silent canyons themselves, even vinegarones and milermore birds. There were bonuses at every bend of the river in spite of edgy nerves and screaming muscles."

By the time the sun had shone a broiling face over the east rim to burn out the rosy mists of canyon dawn, we had cooked and eaten a monumental breakfast of Tang, ham, pancakes, and cocoa, just as if we were sure of rescue before lunch. When all the gear was packed into the empty food boxes and when all discards were buried, Kem and I began the ascent of the dangerously slipping moraine. Every step threatened to start an avalanche. Two hours later a buttermilk sky of cirro-cumulus seemed on the verge of thickening and blotting out the sun. We had no hankering to get caught on that cliff in a cloudburst.

About half way up we came upon a bed of fossils the beauty and perfection of which made us both stop. The echo of our exclamations passed from wall to wall, and the boys on the beach far below looked up to discover what

had happened. The broken strata revealed a veritable petrified marineland whose prehistoric autograph was to be
found mostly in little animals wrapped up in shells. The
farther up we climbed, the greater the variety of these
packages in stone appeared. Mike wanted to collect a
pocketful of different species, so I continued to thread a
precarious route up to the rim where La Vieille was sifting
sand through a small moor of rockrose and rattlepod.

There was no plain or plateau at the summit . . . just
rolling, heaving domes. While cooling off a bit in the wind
before tackling the serious business of photography, I wandered out among the caprock boulders and onto a semi-
precious stone pavement of jasper terrazzo. What an El
Dorado for the rock hound! I fingered striated nodules of
agate, chalcedony, and chert; opalized wood; nuggets of
rose beryl and turquoise; and rubbed the waxy luster of
carnelian—time's sandblasted legacy to anyone who would
make the effort to bend and pick it up. The aborigines had
sat there centuries before and chipped their finest weapon
heads from this natural treasure chest. The mosaics of red
and green jasper hamadas seemed limitless.

Crowning the picturesque overview from the windy
heights were the Sixshooter Peaks to the east, dark pyra-
mids rising from a north-swinging flank of the Orange
Cliffs; while the western wall of The Ledge seemed to play
the rôle of Atlas in supporting the main ribs of the colorful
cliffs on the western horizon. Immediately northwest of the
bowknot course of Stillwater Canyon stood six hundred
square miles of monuments to the silent ages: the Land of
Standing Rocks whose unlichened obelisks and minarets
lifted a thousand fingers as if admiring their own brilliant
prisms of color. The vast vertical peninsula in the center of

the confluence **Y** curtailed the view north, but the gorge of the rivers—these two unscrupulous giants which joined forces those millions of years ago to carve the Grand Canyon into the face of Mother Earth—spread unobstructed below.

After studying the scene for an hour Nineteenth-Century man's geological mistake in nomenclature which shoved the Green aside somehow didn't seem to matter as much as it once did. Perhaps Powell's conclusion—that the Green and the Grand formed the Colorado—was a fair compromise after all. Still in my own mind, the Green would be forever the *fleuve* and the Colorado would be Nature's afterthought *rivière*. The Colorado, draining the entire western flank of the Colorado Rockies, was without question the Green's chief contributor. The canyons of the Green would always remain deeper, followed in order by the Colorado, the San Juan, the Yampa, the Virgin, and the Uintah. Through all her fury, Old Mother Green has been able to cut her trench but little deeper than that of her tributaries. When she reaches the Sea of Cortez, 2300 miles south of her sparkling Wind River cradle, how tiny and insignificant her flowing epic will seem—ingested, gone, and forgotten at Santa Clara el Golfo!

But the river will always return. She will evaporate from the sea, rise into the upper atmosphere, ride the backs of her legions of billowing clouds, descend by tiny crystalline parachutes onto the Wind River Mountains, and so begin her cycle of work all over again.

The warm smell of wet silt drifted up to the rim to remind me of a rendezvous we had at the confluence embayment, although it was beginning to look at if Tex couldn't

The confluence of the Green (left) and Colorado (right) Rivers. Having completed their journey, the three Leaping Thunderbirds rest on their last beach.

make it. The buttermilk formations overhead had lifted into long, strung-out cirro-stratus mackerel. We ought to challenge those first upenders at the head of Cataract Canyon before La Vieille found her way down there to complicate an already bad situation. I took one last sweeping look at the fiercely enchanting distances.

When I returned to the acreage above the box elder thicket, I found Mike Kem exploring for arrowheads. "This flat was an Indian settlement," he assured me. "Broken arrowheads, metates, and pottery all over the place. By the way, there's a herd of bighorns in the ravine around that drop that leads down to Stillwater." Mike was very serious. We were so accustomed to the smile he wore that he seemed almost naked without it. "Bob, Tex isn't coming, is he?"

"Let's go back to camp and load the canoes. To heck with Tex McClatchy!"

The other boys were already resigned to the uncertainties of more days of hazardous rapids, long hours, and short rations when Mike and I walked into camp. "Oh, well," Mike Shannon was saying, "we've all gained weight and grown a couple of inches. It won't hurt us."

No man ever had a finer crew. During the course of the trip, no boy ever came to me with a complaint about another member of the group. Never once did I have to issue a threat for unacceptable behavior; never once did I have to mete out a punishment. Beginning as boys, they weren't always noble, but they were never ignoble. From the first day to the last, it was a teamwork relationship which grew into the stature of the most respectable manhood under the unrelenting tutelage of the very personable river.

We turned the canoes over to shake out the sand before loading. Chip and Joe were parceling out the gear to balance weights; balance was half the battle on the crests.

Suddenly my Indian ears galvanized me in my tracks. "Wait," I whispered. "Listen!"

"Probably an airplane off course," Chip suggested.

"No," Reese said. "That's a jet boat engine."

And a jet it was! On a distant bend of the Colorado the tawny twin roostertails of Tex McClatchy's river craft appeared. "Bet you'd given me up." Tex seemed to laugh out the words in an easy shoalwaterman's drawl. No one volunteered to confess what we were about to do.

"Say, Tex," I heard Mike Kem ask when we were under

way up the Colorado, "have you ever seen a milermore bird?"

"I've heard a lot about 'em, but it's vinegarones you gotta look out for in these parts!"

Until we rounded the bend, I stood at the stern rail looking back for as long as I could see Old Mother Green. We had read her message, partaken of all she had offered us, and brought back with us a part of her wisdom. We know that her song of wild water and the symphonic echoes of her canyon halls will linger in our memories forever.

Glossary

AFT: to the rear

ANASAZI: the cliff dwellers or Ancient Ones

BACKWATER: to paddle backwards to slow down

BANGSTRIP: a metal strip around the bow and stern

BEACH: to go ashore with the canoe

BLADE: the wide part of the paddle

BOX CANYON: a deep, dead-end canyon

BURBLE: a whirlpool in reverse

CANYON STRADIVARIUS: harmonica

CAROME: to stagger—striking things out of control

CATARACT: a rapid-like fall, steeper than a rapid

CHUTE: a straight funnel of water leading into a rapid

CLOSE: to approach and land, generally parallel with the shore

COMBER: a wave with a splashing top

CORDELLE: to walk a boat through a rapid with four ropes attached

COULEE: a steep-walled valley

CREST: a white water wave

CUSP: a pointed peak

DEAD FALL: a tree that has fallen into the river

DEPTH CHARGE: a boulder just under the surface of the water

DINEH: Indian term meaning the people

FLUME: a pipe leading from a dam through which excess water flows

FORE: to the front

GEE: to the right

GUIDON: small flag rigged to point out a complicated course through a rapid

HONDO: a metal ring at the end of a rope

KEEL: longitudinal member along bottom of boat

KEEL SEAM: the attachment of the keel to the bottom

LINE: to guide a canoe through the water with a rope from shore

LIP: the upper spillway of a rapid

LIST: to lean to one side

LOOM: the shank of a canoe paddle

MOKI: an incorrect term referring to cliff dwellers

OATMEAL PONE: a bread baked from boiled oatmeal

PAINTER: bowline or sternline

PLAYA: the riverman's term for beach

PONCHO: rubberized slicker

PORTAGE: carrying of boats or goods overland

PURCHASE: the "bite" or grip the paddle blade has in the water

QUARTER: when wind blows from one side across a body

RIPARIAN: relating to the shores of a river

RUMBADOON: the rumbling noise a rapid makes from a distance

RUN: to shoot or go through; ride out

SCALE: a rapid's rating as to difficulty to maneuver, i.e., scale one
—interesting; scale six—impossible

SCULL: to propel the boat by rotating the paddle off the stern

SECOND-FEET: cubic feet of water per second past a given point

SIFFLE: the noise made against the hull by the water in motion

SHOALWATER: white water—in other words, rapid

SHOOT: to run or ride through a rapid

SLICK: the pool of water leading into a rapid

SLIPOFF: side of a river bank least precipitous

SLOUGH (pronounced "sluff"):   to drag

SLUICE: the water just ahead of the slick before the waves

SNUB: to tie

SQUAW WOOD: brittle dead wood that has not decayed

STEERAGE: reaction of a canoe to position of blade astern

STRING: lining a canoe along the shore to keep from running a
dangerous rapid, generally held by ropes fore and aft

TALUS: a slope that has resulted from weathering of a cliff

THWART: divider running between gunnels (gunwales)

TOPSIDERS: low tennis shoes or deck shoes

TRACK: to walk a canoe through shallow water

TROUGH: the hollow gutter between waves

VEGA: glade

VIGA: beam of a ceiling in cliff dwellings

WAKE: the path of ripples left by a moving vessel

WATERWHEEL: the spinning wave at the bottom of a steep sluice
caused by a secondary obstruction which throws the water in
a circle back upstream

WEDGE: the V-shaped member aft of bow and fore of stern

WEIR: a dam or dike

WHITE WATER: the waves of a rapid

YAW: to turn